C#

A Beginner's Tutorial

Jayden Ky

C#: A Beginner's Tutorial
Copyright © 2013 Brainy Software Inc.
First Edition: September 2013

ISBN: 978-0-9808396-3-0

Book and Cover Designer: Mona Setiadi

Technical Reviewer: Paul Deck
Indexer: Chris Mayle

Trademarks
Oracle and Java are registered trademarks of Oracle and/or its affiliates.
UNIX is a registered trademark of The Open Group.
Microsoft Internet Explorer is either a registered trademark or a trademark of Microsoft Corporation in The United States and/or other countries.
Apache is a trademark of The Apache Software Foundation.
Firefox is a registered trademark of the Mozilla Foundation.
Google is a trademark of Google, Inc.

Throughout this book the printing of trademarked names without the trademark symbol is for editorial purpose only. We have no intention of infringement of the trademark.

Warning and Disclaimer
Every effort has been made to make this book as accurate as possible. The author and the publisher shall have neither liability nor responsibility to any person or entity with respect to any loss or damages arising from the information in this book.

Table of Contents

Introduction

Welcome to *C#: A Beginner's Tutorial*.

C# (pronounced "c sharp") is a mature programming language that is easy to learn. At the same time it is also part of the .NET Framework, a vast collection of technologies that are so diverse that beginners often don't know where to start. If you are one of them, then this book is for you because it has been designed as a tutorial for novices. .NET, by the way, is pronounced "dot net."

As a beginner's tutorial, this book does not teach you every technology there is in the .NET Framework. Rather, this book covers the most important C# and .NET Framework programming topics that you need to master to be able to learn other technologies yourself. Nonetheless this book is comprehensive that by fully understanding all the chapters you should be able to perform an intermediate C# programmer's daily tasks quite well.

This book offers all the three subjects that a professional C# programmer must be proficient in:

- The C# programming language;
- Object-oriented programming (OOP) with C#;
- The .NET Framework class library.

What makes structuring an effective C# course difficult is the fact that the three subjects are interdependent. On the one hand, C# is an OOP language, so its syntax is easier to learn if you already know about OOP. On the other hand, OOP features such as inheritance, polymorphism, and data encapsulation, are best taught if accompanied by real-world examples. Unfortunately, understanding real-world C# programs requires knowledge of the .NET Framework class library.

Because of such interdependence, the three main topics are not grouped into three isolated parts. Instead, chapters discussing a major topic and chapters teaching another are interwoven. For example, before explaining polymorphism, this book makes sure that you are familiar with certain .NET Framework classes so that real-world examples can accompany the polymorphism chapter. In addition, because a language feature such as generics cannot be explained effectively without the comprehension of a certain set of classes, it is covered after the discussion of the supporting classes.

There are also situations whereby a topic can be found in two or more places. For instance, looping statements with **for** and **while** are a basic language feature that should be discussed in an early chapter. However, looping over an array or a collection with **foreach** can only be given after arrays and the collection types are taught. Therefore, looping statements are first presented in Chapter 3, "Statements" and then revisited when we discuss arrays in Chapter 5, "Core Classes" and when we talk about collections in Chapter 13, "Collections."

The rest of this introduction presents a high-level overview of the .NET Framework, an introduction to OOP, a brief description of each chapter, and instructions for installing the .NET Framework.

Overview of the .NET Framework

The .NET Framework is the popular name for a programming environment specification called the Common Language Infrastructure (CLI). The CLI is developed by Microsoft and standardized by ISO and ECMA. Both ISO and ECMA are international standardization bodies.

One of the appeals of the .NET Framework is the fact that it supports multiple programming languages. In fact, on the last count there are more than thirty languages that can target the .NET Framework, including Visual Basic, C#, and C++. This means, if you're used to Visual Basic, you can continue programming in that language and if you're a C++ programmer, you don't have to learn a new language in order to take advantage of what the .NET Framework has to offer.

However, multilanguage support is by no means the only feature of the .NET Framework. It also offers a set of technologies that make software development more rapid and resulting applications more robust and secure. For years the .NET Framework has been the technology of choice because of the benefits it offers:

- cross-language integration
- ease of use
- platform independence
- an extensive class library that speeds up application development
- security
- scalability
- extensive industry support

The .NET Framework is not like a traditional programming environment. In traditional programming, source code is compiled into executable code. This executable code is native to the target platform because it can run only on the platform it is intended to run. In other words, code written and compiled for Windows will only run on Windows, code written in Linux will only run on Linux, and so on. This is depicted in Figure I.1.

Figure I.1: Traditional programming paradigm

By contrast, a .NET Framework program is compiled into Common Intermediate Language (CIL, pronounced "sil" or "kil") code. (If you're familiar with Java, CIL code is equivalent to Java bytecode.) CIL code, formerly known as Microsoft Intermediate Language or MSIL code, can only run on the common language runtime (CLR). The CLR is a native application that interprets CIL code. Because the CLR is available on many platforms, the same CIL code has become cross-platform. As shown in Figure I.2, you can use any supported language to write a .NET program and compile it into CIL code. The very same CIL code can then run on any operating system for which a CLR has been developed. In addition to the CIL code, a .NET compiler also generates metadata that describes the types in the CIL code. This metadata is termed a manifest. Both CIL code and the corresponding manifest are packaged into a .dll or .exe file called an assembly.

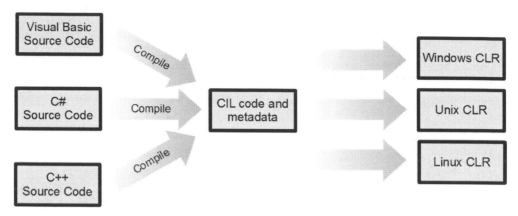

Figure I.2: .NET programming model

Currently Microsoft provides a CLR implementation for Windows, however other implementations from Project Mono (http://www.mono-project.com) and DotGNU Portable.NET (http://dotgnu.org/pnet.html) have meant CIL code can also run on Linux, Mac OS X, BSD, Sony PlayStation 3, and Apple iPhone.

In .NET jargon, code that can only run on top of the CLR is termed managed code. On the other side of the horizon, some .NET languages such as C# and C++ can generate both managed and unmanaged code. Unmanaged code runs outside the runtime. In this book, only managed code is discussed.

When programming C# or other .NET languages, you'll invariably work with the common type system (CTS). Before I explain the CTS, I'd like to make sure you know what a type is. So, what is a type? In computer programming a type determines the kind of value, such as a number or a piece of text. Type information is particularly useful for the compiler. For example, it makes sense to write multiplication **3 * 2** because 3 and 2 are numbers. However, if you write **VB * C#** in your C# code, the compiler will invalidate it because you cannot multiply two pieces of text. At least, not in C#.

In the CTS, there are these five categories of types:

- class
- structure
- enumeration
- interface
- delegate

You will learn each of these types in this book.

An Overview of Object-Oriented Programming

Object-oriented programming (OOP) works by modeling applications on real-world objects. Three principles of OOP are encapsulation, inheritance, and polymorphism.

The benefits of OOP are real. These are the reason why most modern programming languages, including C#, are object-oriented (OO). I can even cite two well-known examples of language transformation to support OOP: The C language evolved into C++ and Visual Basic was upgraded to Visual Basic.NET.

This section explains the benefits of OOP and provides an assessment of how easy or hard it is to learn OOP.

The Benefits of OOP

The benefits of OOP include easy code maintenance, code reuse, and extendibility. These benefits are presented in more detail below.

1. **Ease of maintenance**. Modern software applications tend to be very large. Once upon a time, a "large" system comprised a few thousand lines of code. Now, even those consisting of one million lines are not considered that large. When a system gets larger, it starts giving its developers problems. Bjarne Stroustrup, the father of C++, once said something like this. A small program can be written in anything, anyhow. If you don't quit easily, you'll make it work, at the end. But a large program is a different story. If you don't use techniques of

"good programming," new errors will emerge as fast as you fix the old ones.

The reason for this is there is interdependency among different parts of a large program. When you change something in some part of the program, you may not realize how the change might affect other parts. OOP makes it easy to make applications modular, and modularity makes maintenance less of a headache. Modularity is inherent in OOP because a class, which is a template for objects, is a module by itself. A good design should allow a class to contain similar functionality and related data. An important and related term that is used often in OOP is coupling, which means the degree of interaction between two modules. Loosely coupling among parts make code reuse—another benefit of OOP—easier to achieve.

2. **Reusability**. Reusability means that code that has previously been written can be reused by the code author and others who need the same functionality provided by the original code. It is not surprising then that an OOP language often comes with a set of ready-to-use libraries. In the case of C#, the language is part of the .NET Framework that offers a library of classes that have been carefully designed and tested. It is also easy to write and distribute your own library. Support for reusability in a programming platform is very attractive because it shortens development time.

One of the main challenges to class reusability is creating good documentation for the class library. How fast can a programmer find a class that provides the functionality he/she is looking for? Is it faster to find such a class or write a new one from scratch? Fortunately, the .NET Framework class library comes with extensive documentation.

Reusability does not only apply to the coding phase through the reuse of classes and other types; when designing an application in an OO system, solutions to OO design problems can also be reused. These solutions are called design patterns. To make it easier to refer to each solution, each pattern is given a name. The early catalog of reusable design patterns can be found in the classic book *Design Patterns: Elements of Reusable Object-Oriented Software*, by Erich Gamma, Richard Helm, Ralph Johnson, and John Vlissides.

3. **Extendibility**

Every application is unique. It has its own requirements and specifications. In terms of reusability, sometimes you cannot find an existing class that provides the exact functionality that your application requires. However, you will probably find one or two that provide part of the functionality. Extendibility means that you can still use those classes by extending them to suit your need. You still save time, because you don't have to write code from scratch.

In OOP, extendibility is achieved through inheritance. You can extend an existing class, add some methods or data to it, or change the behavior of methods you don't like. If you know the basic functionality that will be used in many cases, but you don't want your class to provide very specific functions, you can provide a generic class that can be extended later to provide functionality specific to an application.

Is OOP Hard?

C# programmers need to master OOP. As it happens, it does make a difference if you have had programmed using a procedural language, such as C or Pascal. In the light of this, there is bad news and good news.

First the bad news.

Researchers have been debating the best way to teach OOP in school; some argue that it is best to teach procedural programming before OOP is introduced. In many curricula, we see that an OOP course can be taken when a student is nearing the final year of his/her university term.

More recent studies, however, argue that someone with procedural programming skill thinks in a paradigm very different from how OO programmers view and try to solve problems. When this person needs to learn OOP, the greatest struggle he/she faces is having to go through a paradigm shift. It is said that it takes six to 18 months to switch your mindset from procedural to object-oriented paradigms. Another study shows that students who have not learned procedural programming do not find OOP that difficult.

Now the good news.

C# qualifies as one of the easiest OOP languages to learn. For example, you don't have to worry about pointers or spend precious time solving memory leaks caused by failing to destroy unused objects. On top of that, the .NET Framework comes with a very comprehensive class library with relatively very few bugs in their early versions. Once you know the nuts and bolts of OOP, programming with C# is really easy.

About This Book

The following presents the overview of each chapter.

Chapter 1, "Your First Taste of C#" aims at giving you the feel of working with C#. This includes writing a simple C# program, compiling it using the **csc** tool, and running it. In addition, some advice on code conventions and integrated development environments is also given.

Chapter 2, "Language Fundamentals" teaches you the C# language syntax. You will be introduced to topics such as character sets, primitives, variables, operators, etc.

Chapter 3, "Statements" explains C# statements **for**, **while**, **do-while**, **if**, **if-else**, **switch**, **break**, and **continue**.

Chapter 4, "Objects and Classes" is the first OOP lesson in this book. It starts by explaining what a C# object is and how it is stored in memory. It then continues with a discussion of classes, class members, and two OOP concepts (abstraction and encapsulation).

Chapter 5, "Core Classes" covers important classes in the .NET Framework class library: **System.Object**, **System.String**, **System.Text.StringBuilder**, and **System.Console**. Boxing/unboxing and arrays are also taught. This is an important chapter because the classes explained in this chapter are some of the most commonly used classes in the .NET Framework.

Chapter 6, "Inheritance" discusses an OOP feature that enables code extendibility. This chapter teaches you how to extend a class, affect the visibility of a subclass, override a method, and so forth.

Chapter 7, "Structures" explains the second type of the CTS. It also highlights the differences between reference types and value types and talks about some frequently used structures in the .NET Framework class library. This chapter also teaches you how to write your own structures.

Undoubtedly, error handling is an important feature of any programming language. As a mature language, C# has a very robust error handling mechanism that can help prevent bugs from creeping in. Chapter 8, "Error Handling" is a detailed discussion of this mechanism.

Chapter 9, "Numbers and Dates" deals with three issues when working with numbers and dates: parsing, formatting, and manipulation. This chapter introduces .NET types that can help you with these tasks.

Chapter 10, "Interfaces and Abstract Classes" explains that an interface is more than a class without implementation. An interface defines a contract between a service provider and a client. This chapter explains how to work with interfaces and abstract classes.

Chapter 11, "Enumerations" show how to use the keyword **enum** to declare an enumeration. This chapter also demonstrates how to use enumerations in C# programs.

Chapter 12, "Generics" talks about generics.

Chapter 13, "Collections" shows how you can use the members of the **System.Collections.Generic** namespace to group objects and manipulate them.

Chapter 14, "Input/Output" introduces the concept of streams and explains how you can use streams to perform input-output operations.

You'll find Chapter 15, "Windows Presentation Foundation" interesting because you'll learn to write desktop applications, with good-looking user interface and easy-to-use controls.

Polymorphism is one of the main pillars of OOP. It is incredibly useful in situations whereby the type of an object in not known at compile time. Chapter 16, "Polymorphism" explains this feature and provides useful examples.

Accessing databases and manipulating data are some of the most important tasks in business applications. There are many flavors of database servers and accessing different databases requires different skills. Chapter 17, "ADO.NET" explains how to access the database and manipulate relational data in a database.

Appendix A, "Visual Studio Express 2012 for Windows Desktop" discusses a free Integrated Development Environment (IDE) that can help you code more effectively. This tool runs on Windows 7 and Windows 8 and you should consider using it. If you're using an older version of Windows, then your choice of IDE is Visual C# 2010 Express, which is explained in Appendix B, "Visual C# 2010 Express."

Finally, Appendix C, "SQL Server 2012 Express" explains how you can install this free software and create a database.

Downloading and Installing the .NET Framework

Before you can start compiling and running C# programs, you need to download and install the .NET Framework software.

By default, Windows operating systems released after the .NET Framework emerged include a version of the .NET Framework software. However, Windows 7 brings with it .NET Framework 3.5. Therefore, if you need version 4 or 4.5, you need to install it separately. If you plan on using Visual Studio, you're in luck because it includes a version of the .NET Framework and you don't need to install it separately. Otherwise, you can download .NET version 4.5 from this site.

```
http://msdn.microsoft.com/en-us/library/5a4x27ek.aspx
```

To compile from the command line, you need to add the directory containing the csc.exe file (the C# compiler) to your PATH environment variable. The directory is C:\Windows\Microsoft.NET\Framework\v4.x.y, where x and y are release numbers. The actual values of x and y depend on your installation. For instance, the version on my computer is 4.0.30319.

Alternatively, if you're on a 64bit computer, you may have this directory: C:\Windows\Microsoft.NET\Framework64\v4.x.y.

To add a directory to your **PATH** variable, right-click on the **My Computer** icon on your desktop and select the **Properties** menu option. From the resulting dialog box, click the **Environment Variables** button located under the **Advanced** tab or **Advanced system settings** tab. From that resulting dialog box, add the following directory listings at the end of the current **Path** variable found in the **System** variables list box (note that each entry must be separated by a semicolon).

Choosing An IDE

An integrated development environment (IDE) is a must-have tool that every programmer should use. Most modern IDEs significantly increase productivity by helping programmers find bugs earlier and debug and trace their programs.

In terms of .NET Framework development, there are a couple of IDEs available, but Microsoft Visual Studio is a clear winner. And fortunately, a stripped-down version of Visual Studio, Visual Studio Express 2012 for Windows Desktop (for Windows 7 and 8 users) and Visual C# 2010 Express (for earlier versions of Windows), are available for free. You should now download and install an IDE if you have not done so. You will also need to register your software to continue using it after your first use. Registration is free.

Downloading Program Examples

The program examples accompanying this book and answers to the questions in each chapter can be downloaded from this URL:

```
http://books.brainysoftware.com
```

Extract the zip file to a working directory and you're good to start your C# programming journey.

Chapter 1
Your First Taste of C#

Developing a C# program involves writing code, compiling it into Common Intermediate Language (CIL) code, and running the CIL code. This is a process you will repeat again and again during your career as a C# programmer, and it is crucial that you feel comfortable with it. Therefore, the main objective of this chapter is to give you the opportunity to experience the process of software development in C# using Visual Studio Express 2012 for Windows Desktop or Visual C# 2010 Express, two free Integrated Development Environments (IDEs) from Microsoft.

As it is important to write code that not only works but that is also easy to read and maintain, this chapter introduces you to C# code conventions. Examples for this and following chapters are assumed to be developed in Visual Studio Express 2012 for Windows Desktop or Visual C# 2010 Express.

Your First C# Program

This section highlights steps in C# development: writing the program, compiling it into CIL code, and running the CIL code. You will be using Visual Studio Express 2012 for Windows Desktop or Visual C# 2010 Express, which can be downloaded for free from Microsoft's website. If you have not done so, please install one of these tools. Visual Studio Express 2012 for Windows Desktop is for you if you're using Windows 7 or Windows 8. Otherwise, download and install Visual C# 2010 Express. Please refer to Appendix A, "Visual Studio Express 2012 for Windows Desktop" or Appendix B, "Visual C# 2010 Express."

Starting Your IDE

Start your IDE. When opened, you'll see something similar to Figure 1.1 or Figure 1.2. If the software won't open because you have not registered, you should do it now. Registration is free and easy and explained in Appendix A and Appendix B.

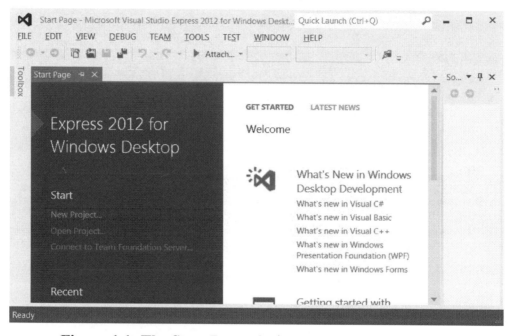

Figure 1.1: The Start Page of Visual Studio Express 2012

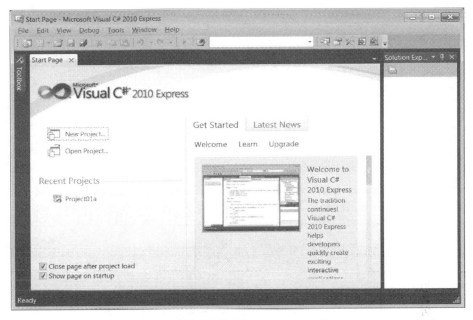

Figure 1.2: Visual C# 2010 Express, ready to serve you

The windows for both IDEs look different but offer similar functionality. From now on, I'll be only showing screenshots from Visual C# 2010 Express.

Click the **New Project** icon to create a new project and select **Console Application** (See Figure 1.3).

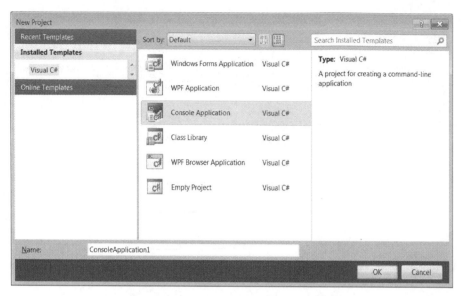

Figure 1.3: Creating a new project

Accept **ConsoleApplication1** as the solution and project names, then click the **OK** button. You'll see a project and a solution created for you like in Figure 1.4. Better still, Visual C# 2010 Express also creates a program file with some boilerplate code like the one in Figure 1.3. Note that a project is a container to easily manage your application. It contains C# source files and other resources such as image and video files and documentation that describes your application. When you create a project, Visual C# 2010 Express also creates a solution. A solution is yet another container that may contain one or more projects.

Now you're ready to program.

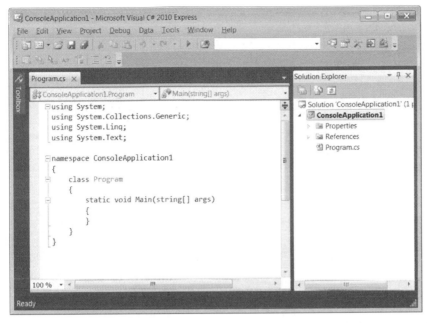

Figure 1.4: The created solution and project

Writing a C# Program

Insert the following two lines after the opening curly bracket after **static void Main(string[] args)**:

```
Console.WriteLine("Hello World!");
Console.ReadLine();
```

Listing 1.1 shows your complete program with recently inserted lines printed in bold.

Listing 1.1: A simple C# program

```
using System;
using System.Collections.Generic;
using System.Linq;
using System.Text;

namespace ConsoleApplication1
{
    class Program
```

```
    {
        static void Main(string[] args)
        {
            Console.WriteLine("Hello World!");
            Console.ReadLine();
        }
    }
}
```

Alternatively, you can double-click on the solution (.sln) file in the zip file accompanying this book that you can download from the book's download site.

Compiling and Running Your C# Program

Developing with Visual C# 2010 Express is really easy. To compile your program, simply press the F5 key or click the Start button on the toolbar. The Start button is green and is shown in Figure 1.5.

Figure 1.5: The Start button

If your program compiled successfully, Visual C# 2010 Express will also run your program. As a result, you'll see a console with the text "Hello World!" See Figure 1.6.

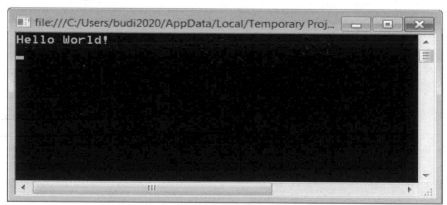

Figure 1.6: Running your program

Congratulations. You have successfully written your first C# program. Type Enter to close the console after you finish admiring your first program. Since the sole aim of this chapter is to familiarize yourself with the writing and compiling process, I will not be attempting to explain how the program works.

C# Code Conventions

It is important to write correct C# programs that run. However, it is also crucial to write programs that are easy to read and maintain. It is believed that eighty percent of the lifetime cost of a piece of software is spent on maintenance. Also, the turnover of programmers is high, thus it is very likely that someone other than you will maintain your code during its lifetime. Whoever inherits your code will appreciate clear and easy-to-read program sources.

Using consistent code conventions is one way to make your code easier to read. (Other ways include proper code organization and sufficient commenting.) Code conventions include filenames, file organization, indentation, comments, declaration, statements, white space, and naming conventions. Microsoft has published a document that outlines standards that its employees should follow. The document can be viewed here.

```
http://msdn.microsoft.com/en-us/library/ff926074.aspx
```

Program samples in this book will follow the recommended conventions outlined in this document. I'd also like to encourage you to develop the habit of following these conventions starting the first day of your programming career, so that writing clear code comes naturally at a later stage.

Summary

This chapter helped you write your first C# program using Visual Studio Express 2012 for Windows Desktop or Visual C# 2010 Express. You successfully wrote, compiled, and ran your program.

Chapter 2
Language Fundamentals

C# is an object-oriented programming (OOP) language, therefore an understanding of OOP is of utmost importance. Chapter 4, "Objects and Classes" is the first lesson of OOP in this book. However, before you explore many features and techniques in OOP, make sure you study the prerequisite: basic programming concepts discussed in this chapter. The topics covered are as follows.

- Encoding Sets. C# supports the Unicode character encoding set and program element names are not restricted to ASCII (American Standard Code for Information Interchange) characters. Text can be written using characters in practically any human language in use today.
- Intrinsic types. Each of these types is a short name or alias for a type in the .NET class library. For example, **int** is the short name for the **System.Int32** structure.
- Variables. Variables are place holders whose contents can change. There are many types of variables.
- Constants. Place holders whose values cannot be changed.
- Literals. Literals are representations of data values that are understood by the C# compiler.
- Type conversion. Changing the type of a data type to another type.
- Operators. Operators are notations indicating that certain operations are to be performed.

Note
If you have programmed with Java or C++, two popular languages at the time C# was invented, you should feel at home learning C# because C# syntax is very similar to that of Java and C++. However,

the creator of C# added a number of features not available in Java and C++ and excluded a few aspects of them.

ASCII and Unicode

Traditionally, computers in English speaking countries only used the ASCII (American Standard Code for Information Interchange) character set to represent alphanumeric characters. Each character in the ASCII is represented by seven bits. There are therefore 128 characters in this character set. These include the lower case and upper case Latin letters, numbers, and punctuation marks.

The ASCII character set was later extended to include another 128 characters, such as the German characters ä, ö, ü, and the British currency symbol £. This character set is called extended ASCII and each character is represented by eight bits.

ASCII and the extended ASCII are only two of the many character sets available. Another popular one is the character set standardized by the ISO (International Standards Organization), ISO-8859-1, also known as Latin-1. Each character in ISO-8859-1 is represented by eight bits as well. This character set contains all the characters required for writing text in many of the western European languages, such as German, Danish, Dutch, French, Italian, Spanish, Portuguese, and, of course, English. An eight-bit-per-character character set is convenient because a byte is also eight bits long. As such, storing and transmitting text written in an 8-bit character set is most efficient.

However, not every language uses Latin letters. Chinese, Korean, and Thai are examples of languages that use different character sets. For example, each character in the Chinese language represents a word, not a letter. There are thousands of these characters and eight bits are not enough to represent all the characters in the character set. The Japanese use a different character set for their language too. In total, there are hundreds of different character sets for all languages in the world. This is confusing, because a code that represents a particular character in a character set represents a different character in another character set.

Unicode is a character set developed by a non-profit organization called the Unicode Consortium (www.unicode.org). This body attempts to include all characters in all languages in the world into one single character set. A unique number in Unicode represents exactly one character. Currently at version 6, Unicode is used in the .NET Framework, Java, XML, ECMAScript, LDAP, etc. It has also been adopted by industry leaders such as IBM, Microsoft, Oracle, Google, HP, Apple, and others.

Initially, a Unicode character was represented by sixteen bits, which were enough to represent more than 65,000 different characters. 65,000 characters are sufficient for encoding most of the characters in major languages in the world. However, the Unicode consortium planned to allow for encoding for as many as a million more characters. With this amount, you then need more than sixteen bits to represent each character. In fact, a 32 bit system is considered a convenient way of storing Unicode characters.

Now, you see a problem already. While Unicode provides enough space for all the characters used in all languages, storing and transmitting Unicode text is not as efficient as storing and transmitting ASCII or Latin-1 characters. In the Internet world, this is a huge problem. Imagine having to transfer 4 times as much data as ASCII text!

Fortunately, character encoding can make it more efficient to store and transmit Unicode text. You can think of character encoding as analogous to data compression. And, there are many types of character encodings available today. The Unicode Consortium endorses three of them:

- UTF-8 (Unicode Transformation Format, 8-bit encoding form). This is popular for HTML and for protocols whereby Unicode characters are transformed into a variable length encoding of bytes. It has the advantages that the Unicode characters corresponding to the familiar ASCII set have the same byte values as ASCII, and that Unicode characters transformed into UTF-8 can be used with much existing software. Most browsers support the UTF-8 character encoding.
- UTF-16 (Unicode Transformation Format, 16-bit encoding form). In this character encoding, all the more commonly used characters fit into a single 16-bit code unit, and other less often used characters are accessible via pairs of 16-bit code units. The .NET Framework uses this character encoding.

- UTF-32 (Unicode Transformation Format, 32-bit encoding form). This character encoding uses 32 bits for every single character. This is clearly not a choice for Internet applications. At least, not at present.

ASCII characters still play a dominant role in software programming. C# too uses ASCII for almost all input elements, except comments, identifiers, and the contents of characters and strings. For the latter, C# supports Unicode characters. This means, you can write comments, identifiers, and strings in languages other than English. For example, if you are a Chinese speaker living in Beijing, you can use Chinese characters for variable names. As a comparison, here is a piece of C# code that declares an identifier named **password**, which consists of ASCII characters:

```
string password = "secret";
```

By contrast, the following identifier is in simplified Chinese characters.

```
string 密码 = "secret";
```

Intrinsic Types and the Common Type System

C# is a strongly typed language, which means every piece of data must have a type. This applies to data holders like variables too. C# defines various types known as intrinsic types.

In the meantime, the .NET Framework supports multiple programming languages and code written in one language may interoperate with code written in other languages. In order to facilitate this language interoperability, the .NET Framework designer defines the Common Type System (CTS). The CTS specifies all data types supported by the runtime (that is, the CLR). A requirement for a program written in one language to be used by programs written in other languages is that the former should only expose CTS-compliant types.

C# is rich enough to support intrinsic data types that are both CTS-compliant and CTS-noncompliant. However, C# codes that expose non-CTS-compliant data types may not interoperate well with codes written in another language.

Table 2.1 lists C# intrinsic types.

C# Type	.NET Type	Size (bytes)	Values/Range
byte	Byte	1	0 to 255.
char	Char	2	Any Unicode character.
bool	Boolean	1	true or false.
sbyte*	SByte	1	-128 to 127.
short	Int16	2	-32,768 to 32,767.
ushort*	UInt16	2	0 to 65,535.
int	Int32	4	-2,147,483,648 to 2,147,483,647
uint*	UInt32	4	0 to 4,294,967,295
float	Single	4	-3.402823e38 to 3.402823e38
double	Double	8	-1.79769313486232e308 to 1.79769313486232e308
decimal	Decimal	16	$\pm 1.0 \times 10e-28$ to $\pm 7.9 \times 10e28$
long	Int64	4	-9,223,372,036,854,775,808 to 9,223,372,036,854,775,807
ulong*	UInt64	4	0 to 18446744073709551615
string	String		A sequence of characters
object	Object		Base type of all other types

Table 2.1: C# intrinsic types

The four intrinsic types with an asterisk (**sbyte**, **ushort**, **uint**, **ulong**) are not CTS-compliant, which means other languages may have problems consuming them. Use non-CTS-compliant types with caution.

Beginners often have difficulty choosing a data type. However, it's not hard. The first rule is you have to determine if the type is a number or a non-number. If it is a non-number, then you can choose either **bool**, **char**, or **string**. A **bool** is for something that has two states, such as true/false or yes/no. A **char** type can contain a single Unicode character, such as 'a', '9', or '&'. The use of Unicode allows **char**s to also contain characters that do not exist in the English alphabet, such as this Japanese character 'の'. A string is for a sequence of characters and **string** is one of the most frequently used data types in programming.

For example, **bool** is a good candidate to indicate whether or not a certain product is used. In C# you would write

```
bool used;
```

However, if a product can be in one of three conditions (new, used, and unknown), you cannot use **bool** as three states are too many for this data type. Instead, you might want to use a numeric type, such as **byte**.

The second rule in choosing a data type is you want to use a type with the smallest size. This is especially true for numeric types. **byte**, **sbyte** and **int** can all hold whole numbers. However, if it is for holding a number less than ten, you may want to choose **byte** or **sbyte** because they only use one byte whereas **int** takes four bytes.

In addition, if a value cannot be negative, choose an unsigned type. For instance, use **byte** instead of **sbyte** for age.

```
byte Age;
```

In this case, **byte** is good enough because no one lives to 200. On the other hand, to represent a country population, you may want to use an **int**. But wait, isn`t it a signed data type and the number of people in a country cannot be negative? Yes, but the closest alternative is **uint**, which is not CTS-compliant. I would avoid using any of non-CTS types even if it would cost more to use another data type. If I were to choose a data type that can hold any number between zero and four billion, I'd use **long** (eight bytes width) instead of **uint** (four bytes width) unless memory is a big issue.

The data types **byte**, **short**, **int**, and **long** can only hold integers or whole numbers, for numbers with decimal points you need either a **float** or a **double**.

Variables

Variables are data placeholders. C# is a strongly typed language, therefore every variable must have a declared type. There are two data types in C#:

- reference types. A variable of reference type provides a reference to an object.
- primitive types. A variable of primitive type holds a primitive.

In addition to the data type, a C# variable also has a name or an identifier. There are a few ground rules in choosing identifiers.

1. An identifier is an unlimited-length sequence of letters and digits. An identifier must begin with a letter or an underscore.
2. An identifier must not be a C# keyword (given in Table 2.2), a **bool** literal, or the **null** literal.
3. It must be unique within its scope. Scopes are discussed in Chapter 4, "Objects and Classes."

abstract	do	in	protected	true
as	double	int	public	try
base	else	interface	readonly	typeof
bool	enum	internal	ref	uint
break	event	is	return	ulong
byte	explicit	lock	sbyte	unchecked
case	extern	long	sealed	unsafe
catch	false	namespace	short	ushort
char	finally	new	sizeof	using
checked	fixed	null	stackalloc	virtual
class	float	object	static	void
const	for	operator	string	volatile
continue	foreach	out	struct	while
decimal	goto	override	switch	
default	if	params	this	
delegate	implicit	private	throw	

Table 2.2: C# keywords

Note
You can use a keyword as an identifier if you prefix it with @.

Here are some legal identifiers:

```
salary
x2
_x3
@class
row_count
密码
```

Here are some invalid variables:

```
2x
class
c#+variable
```

2x is invalid because it starts with a number. **class** is a keyword and **c#+variable** is invalid because it contains an asterisk and a plus sign.

Also note that names are case-sensitive. **x2** and **X2** are two different identifiers.

You declare a variable by writing the type first, followed by the name plus a semicolon. Here are some examples of variable declarations.

```
byte x;
int rowCount;
char c;
```

In the examples above you declare three variables:

- The variable **x** of type **byte**
- The variable **rowCount** of type **int**
- The variable **c** of type **char**

x, **rowCount**, and **c** are variable names or identifiers.

It is also possible to declare multiple variables having the same type on the same line, separating two variables with a comma. For instance:

```
int a, b;
```

which is the same as

```
int a;
int b;
```

However, writing multiple declarations on the same line is not recommended as it reduces readability.

Finally, it is possible to assign a value to a variable at the same time the variable is declared:

```
byte x = 12;
int rowCount = 1000;
char c = 'x';
```

Constants

In C# you can prefix a variable declaration with the keyword **const** to make its value unchangeable. For example, the number of months in a year never changes, so you can write:

```
const int NumberOfMonths = 12;
```

As another example, in a class that performs mathematical calculation, you can declare the variable **pi** whose value is equal to 22/7 (the circumference of a circle divided by its diameter, in math represented by the Greek letter π).

```
const float pi = (float) 22 / 7;
```

Once assigned a value, the value cannot change. Attempting to change it will result in a compile error.

Note that the casting **(float)** after **22 / 7** is needed to convert the value of division to **float**. Otherwise, an **int** will be returned and the **pi** variable will have a value of 3, instead of 3.142857.

Also note that since C# uses Unicode characters, you can simply define the variable **pi** as π if you don't think typing it is harder than typing **pi**.

```
const float π = (float) 22 / 7;
```

Literals

From time to time you will need to assign values to variables in your program, such as number 2 to an **int** or the character 'c' to a **char**. For this, you need to write the value representation in a format that the C# compiler understands. This source code representation of a value is called *literal*. There are three types of literals: literals of primitive types, string literals, and the **null** literal. Only literals of primitive types are discussed in this chapter. The **null** literal is discussed in Chapter 4, "Objects and Classes" and string literals in Chapter 5, "Core Classes."

Literals of primitive types have four subtypes: integer literals, floating-point literals, character literals, and bool literals. Each of these subtypes is explained below.

Integer Literals

Integer literals may be written in decimal (base 10, something we are used to), hexadecimal (base 16), or octal (base 8). For example, one hundred can be expressed as **100**. The following are integer literals in decimal:

```
2
123456
```

As another example, the following code assigns 10 to variable **x** of type **int**.

```
int x = 10;
```

Hexadecimal integers are written by using the prefixes **0x** or **0X**. For example, the hexadecimal number 9E is written as 0X9E or 0x9E. Octal integers are written by prefixing the numbers with 0. For instance, the following is an octal number 567:

```
0567
```

Integer literals are used to assign values to variables of types **byte**, **short**, **int**, and **long**. Note, however, you must not assign a value that exceeds the capacity of a variable. For instance, the highest number for a **byte** is 255. Therefore, the following code generates a compile error because 500 is too big for a **byte**.

```
byte b = 500;
```

Note that a long can be suffixed with L.

```
long productId = 9876543210L;
```

Floating-Point Literals

Numbers such as 0.4, 1.23, $0.5e^{10}$ are floating point numbers. A floating point number has the following parts:

- a whole number part
- a decimal point
- a fractional part
- an optional exponent

Take 1.23 as an example. For this floating point, the whole number part is 1, the fractional part is 23, and there is no optional exponent. In $0.5e^{10}$, 0 is the whole number part, 5 the fractional part, and 10 is the exponent.

In the .NET Framework, there are two types of floating points, **float** and **double**. In both **float**s and **double**s, a whole number part of 0 is optional. In other words, 0.5 can be written as .5. Also, the exponent can be represented by either e or E.

To express float literals, you use one of the following formats.

```
Digits . [Digits] [ExponentPart] f_or_F
. Digits [ExponentPart] f_or_F
Digits ExponentPart f_or_F
Digits [ExponentPart] f_or_F
```

Note that the part in brackets is optional.

The *f_or_F* part makes a floating point literal a **float**. The absence of this part makes a float literal a **double**. To explicitly express a double literal, you can suffix it with D or d.

To write double literals, use one of these formats.

```
Digits . [Digits] [ExponentPart] [d_or_D]
. Digits [ExponentPart] [d_or_D]
Digits ExponentPart [d_or_D]
```

```
Digits [ExponentPart] [d_or_D]
```

In both floats and doubles, *ExponentPart* is defined as follows.

```
ExponentIndicator SignedInteger
```

where *ExponentIndicator* is either **e** or **E** and *SignedInteger* is .

$Sign_{opt}$ `Digits`

and *Sign* is either + or - and a plus sign is optional.

Examples of **float** literals include the following:

```
2e1f
8.F
.5f
0F
3.14f
9.0001e+12F
```

Here are examples of **double** literals:

```
2e1
8.
.5
0.0D
3.14
9e-9d
7e123D
```

Bool Literals

The **bool** type has two values, represented by literals **true** and **false**. For example, the following code declares a **bool** variable **includeSign** and assigns it the value of **true**.

```
boolean includeSign = true;
```

Character Literals

A character literal is a Unicode character or an escape sequence enclosed in single quotes. An escape sequence is the representation of a Unicode character that cannot be entered using the keyboard or that has a special function in C#. For example, the carriage return and linefeed characters are used to terminate a line and do not have visual representation. To express a linefeed character, you need to escape it, i.e. write its character representation. Also, single quote characters need to be escaped because single quotes are used to enclosed characters.

Here are some examples of character literals:

```
'a'
'z'
'A'
'Z'
'0'
'ü'
'%'
'我'
```

Here are character literals that are escape sequences:

```
'\b'    the backspace character
'\t'    the tab character
'\\'    the backslash
'\''    single quote
'\"'    double quote
'\n'    linefeed
'\r'    carriage return
```

In addition, C# allows you to escape a Unicode character so that you can express a Unicode character using a sequence of ASCII characters. For example, the Unicode code for the character ⊙ is 2299. You can write the following character literal to express this character:

```
'⊙'
```

However, if you do not have the tool to produce that character using your keyboard, you can escape it like so:

```
'\u2299'
```

Primitive Conversions

When dealing with different data types, you often need to perform conversions. For example, assigning the value of a variable to another variable involves a conversion. If both variables have the same type, the assignment will always succeed. Conversion from a type to the same type is called identity conversion. For example, the following operation is guaranteed to be successful:

```
int a = 90;
int b = a;
```

However, conversion to a different type is not guaranteed to be successful or even possible. There are two other kinds of primitive conversions, the widening conversion and the narrowing conversion.

The Widening Conversion

The widening primitive conversion occurs from one type to another type whose size is the same or larger than that of the first type, such as from **int** (32 bits) to **long** (64 bits). The widening conversion is permitted in the following cases:

- **byte** to **short, int, long, float**, or **double**
- **short** to **int, long, float**, or **double**
- **char** to **int, long, float**, or **double**
- **int** to **long, float**, or **double**
- **long** to **float** or **double**
- **float** to **double**

A widening conversion from an integer type to another integer type will not risk information loss. At the same token, a conversion from **float** to **double** preserves all the information. However, a conversion from an **int** or a **long** to a **float** may result in loss of precision.

The widening primitive conversion occurs implicitly. You do not need to do anything in your code. For example:

```
int a = 10;
long b = a; // widening conversion
```

The Narrowing Conversion

The narrowing conversion occurs from a type to a different type that has a smaller size, such as from a **long** (64 bits) to an **int** (32 bits). In general, the narrowing primitive conversion can occur in these cases:

- **short** to **byte** or **char**
- **char** to **byte** or **short**
- **int** to **byte**, **short**, or **char**
- **long** to **byte**, **short**, or **char**
- **float** to **byte**, **short**, **char**, **int**, or **long**
- **double** to **byte**, **short**, **char**, **int**, **long**, or **float**

Unlike the widening primitive conversion, the narrowing primitive conversion must be explicit. You need to specify the target type in parentheses. For example, here is a narrowing conversion from **long** to **int**.

```
long a = 10;
int b = (int) a; // narrowing conversion
```

The **(int)** on the second line tells the compiler that a narrowing conversion should occur.

The narrowing conversion may incur information loss, if the converted value is larger than the capacity of the target type. The preceding example did not cause information loss because 10 is small enough for an **int**. However, in the following conversion, there is some information loss because 9876543210L is too big for an **int**.

```
long a = 9876543210L;
int b = (int) a; // the value of b is now 1286608618
```

A narrowing conversion that results in information loss introduces a defect in your program.

Operators

A computer program is a collection of operations that together achieve a certain function. There are many types of operations, including addition, subtraction, multiplication, division, and bit shifting. In this section you will learn various C# operators.

An operator performs an operation on one, two, or three operands. Operands are the objects of an operation and the operator is a symbol representing the action. For example, here is an additive operation:

```
x + 4
```

In this case, **x** and 4 and the operands and + is the operator.

An operator may or may not return a result.

Note
Any legal combination of operators and operands are called an expression. For example, **x + 4** is an expression. A boolean expression results in either **true** or **false**. An integer expression produces an integer. And, the result of a floating-point expression is a floating point number.

Operators that require only one operand are called unary operators. There are a few unary operators in C#. Binary operators, the most common type of C# operator, take two operands. There is also one ternary operator, the **? :** operator, that requires three operands.

Table 2.3 list C# operators.

=	>	<	!	~	?	:			
==	<=	>=	!=	&&	||	++	--		
+	-	*	/	&	|	^	%	<<	>>	>>>
+=	-=	*=	/=	&=	|=	^=	%=	<<=	>>=	>>>=

Table 2.3: C# operators

In C#, there are six categories of operators.

- Unary operators
- Arithmetic operators

- Relational and conditional operators
- Shift and logical operators
- Assignment operators
- Other operators

Each of these operators is discussed in the following sections.

Unary Operators

Unary operators operate on one operand. There are six unary operators, all discussed in this section.

Unary Minus Operator –

The unary minus operator returns the negative of its operand. The operand must be a numeric primitive or a variable of a numeric primitive type. For example, in the following code, the value of **y** is -4.5;

```
float x = 4.5f;
float y = -x;
```

Unary Plus Operator +

This operator returns the value of its operand. The operand must be a numeric primitive or a variable of a numeric primitive type. For example, in the following code, the value of **y** is 4.5.

```
float x = 4.5f;
float y - +x;
```

This operator does not have much significance since its absence makes no difference.

Increment Operator ++

This operator increments the value of its operand by one. The operand must be a variable of a numeric primitive type. The operator can appear before or after the operand. If the operator appears before the operand, it is called the prefix increment operator. If it is written after the operand, it becomes the postfix increment operator.

As an example, here is a prefix increment operator in action:

```
int x = 4;
++x;
```

After **++x**, the value of **x** is 5. The preceding code is the same as

```
int x = 4;
x++;
```

After **x++**, the value of **x** is 5.

However, if the result of an increment operator is assigned to another variable in the same expression, there is a difference between the prefix operator and its postfix twin. Consider this example.

```
int x = 4;
int y = ++x;
// y = 5, x = 5
```

The prefix increment operator is applied *before* the assignment. **x** is incremented to 5, and then its value is copied to **y**.

However, check the use of the postfix increment operator here.

```
int x = 4;
int y = x++;
// y = 4, x = 5
```

With the postfix increment operator, the value of the operand (**x**) is incremented *after* the value of the operand is assigned to another variable (**y**).

Note that the increment operator is most often applied to **int**s. However, it also works with other types of numeric primitives, such as **float** and **long**.

Decrement Operator --

This operator decrements the value of its operand by one. The operand must be a variable of a numeric primitive type. Like the increment operator, there are also the prefix decrement operator and the postfix decrement operator. For instance, the following code decrements **x** and assigns the value to **y**.

```
int x = 4;
int y = --x;
// x = 3; y = 3
```

In the following example, the postfix decrement operator is used:

```
int x = 4;
int y = x--;
// x = 3; y = 4
```

Logical Complement Operator !

This operator can only be applied to a **bool** primitive or an instance of **System.Boolean**. The value of this operator is **true** if the operand is **false**, and **false** if the operand is **true**. For example:

```
bool x = false;
bool y = !x;
// at this point, y is true and x is false
```

Bitwise Complement Operator ~

The operand of this operator must be an integer primitive or a variable of an integer primitive type. The result is the bitwise complement of the operand. For example:

```
int j = 2;
int k = ~j; // k = -3; j = 2
```

To understand how this operator works, you need to convert the operand to a binary number and reverse all the bits. The binary form of 2 in an integer is:

```
0000 0000 0000 0000 0000 0000 0000 0010
```

Its bitwise complement is

```
1111 1111 1111 1111 1111 1111 1111 1101
```

which is the representation of -3 in an integer.

sizeof Operator

This unary operator is used to obtain the size of a data type in bytes. For example, **sizeof(int)** returns 4.

Arithmetic Operators

There are four types of arithmetic operations: addition, subtraction, multiplication, division, and modulus. Each arithmetic operator is discussed here.

Addition Operator +

The addition operator adds two operands. The types of the operands must be convertible to a numeric primitive. For example:

```
byte x = 3;
int y = x + 5; // y = 8
```

Make sure the variable that accepts the addition result has a big enough capacity. For example, in the following code the value of **k** is -294967296 and not 4 billion.

```
int j = 2000000000; // 2 billion
int k = j + j; // not enough capacity. A bug!!!
```

On the other hand, the following works as expected:

```
long j = 2000000000; // 2 billion
long k = j + j; // the value of k is 4 billion
```

Subtraction Operator –

This operator performs subtraction between two operands. The types of the operands must be convertible to a numeric primitive type. As an example:

```
int x = 2;
int y = x - 1;      // y = 1
```

Multiplication Operator *

This operator perform multiplication between two operands. The type of the operands must be convertible to a numeric primitive type. As an example:

```
int x = 4;
int y = x * 4;      // y = 16
```

Division Operator /

This operator perform division between two operands. The left hand operand is the dividend and the right hand operand the divisor. Both the dividend and the divisor must be of a type convertible to a numeric primitive type. As an example:

```
int x = 4;
int y = x / 2;      // y = 2
```

Note that at runtime a division operation raises an error if the divisor is zero.

The result of a division using the / operator is always an integer. If the divisor does not divide the dividends equally, the remainder will be ignored. For example

```
int x = 4;
int y = x / 3;      // y = 1
```

Modulus Operator %

This operator perform division between two operands and returns the remainder. The left hand operand is the dividend and the right hand operand the divisor. Both the dividend and the divisor must be of a type that is convertible to a numeric primitive type. For example the result of the following operation is 2.

```
8 % 3
```

Equality Operators

There are two equality operators, == (equal to) and != (not equal to), both operating on two operands that can be integers, floating points, characters, or **bool**. The outcome of equality operators is a **boolean**.

For example, the value of **c** is **true** after the comparison.

```
int a = 5;
int b = 5;
bool c = a == b;
```

As another example,

```
bool x = true;
bool y = true;
bool z = x != y;
```

The value of **z** is **false** after comparison because **x** is equal to **y**.

Relational Operators

There are five relational operators: <, >, <=, and >=. Each of these operators is explained in this section.

The <, >, <=, and >= operators operate on two operands whose types must be convertible to a numeric primitive type. Relational operations return a **bool**.

The < operator evaluates if the value of the left-hand operand is less than the value of the right-hand operand. For example, the following operation returns **false**:

```
9 < 6
```

The > operator evaluates if the value of the left-hand operand is greater than the value of the right-hand operand. For example, this operation returns **true**:

```
9 > 6
```

The <= operator tests if the value of the left-hand operand is less than or equal to the value of the right-hand operand. For example, the following operation evaluates to **false**:

```
9 <= 6
```

The >= operator tests if the value of the left-hand operand is greater than or equal to the value of the right-hand operand. For example, this operation returns **true**:

```
9 >= 9
```

Conditional Operators

There are three conditional operators: the AND operator **&&**, the OR operator ||, and the **? :** operator. Each of these is detailed below.

The && operator

This operator takes two expressions as operands and both expressions must return a value that must be convertible to **bool**. It returns **true** if both operands evaluate to **true**. Otherwise, it returns **false**. If the left-hand operand evaluates to **false**, the right-hand operand will not be evaluated. For example, the following returns **false**.

```
(5 < 3) && (6 < 9)
```

The || Operator

This operator takes two expressions as operands and both expressions must return a value that must be convertible to **bool**. || returns **true** if one of the operands evaluates to **true**. If the left-hand operand evaluates to **true**, the right-hand operand will not be evaluated. For instance, the following returns **true**.

```
(5 < 3) || (6 < 9)
```

The ? : Operator

This operator operates on three operands. The syntax is

```
expression1 ? expression2 : expression3
```

Here, *expression1* must return a value convertible to **boolean**. If *expression1* evaluates to **true**, *expression2* is returned. Otherwise, *expression3* is returned.

For example, the following expression assigns 4 to **x**.

```
int x = (8 < 4) ? 2 : 4
```

Shift Operators

A shift operator takes two operands whose type must be convertible to an integer primitive. The left-hand operand is the value to be shifted, the right-hand operand indicates the shift distance. There are three types of shift operators:

- the left shift operator <<
- the right shift operator >>
- the unsigned right shift operator >>>

The Left Shift Operator <<

The left shift operator bit-shifts a number to the left, padding the right bits with 0. The value of **n** << **s** is **n** left-shifted **s** bit positions. This is the same as multiplication by two to the power of s.

For example, left-shifting an **int** whose value is 1 with a shift distance of 3 (1 << 3) results in 8. Again, to figure this out, you convert the operand to a binary number.

```
0000 0000 0000 0000 0000 0000 0000 0001
```

Shifting to the left 3 shift units results in:

```
0000 0000 0000 0000 0000 0000 0000 1000
```

which is equivalent to 8 (the same as $1 * 2^3$).

Another rule is this. If the left-hand operand is an **int**, only the first five bits of the shift distance will be used. In other words, the shift distance must be within the range 0 and 31. If you pass an number greater than 31, only the first five bits will be used. This is to say, if **x** is an **int**, **x << 32** is the same as **x << 0**; **x << 33** is the same as **x << 1**.

If the left-hand operand is a **long**, only the first six bits of the shift distance will be used. In other words, the shift distance actually used is within the range 0 and 63.

The Right Shift Operator >>

The right shift operator >> bit-shifts the left-hand operand to the right. The value of **n >> s** is **n** right-shifted **s** bit positions. The resulting value is $n/2^s$.

As an example, **16 >> 1** is equal to 8. To prove this, write the binary representation of 16.

```
0000 0000 0000 0000 0000 0000 0001 0000
```

Then, shifting it to the right by 1 bit results in.

```
0000 0000 0000 0000 0000 0000 0000 1000
```

which is equal to 8.

The Unsigned Right Shift Operator >>>

The value of **n >>> s** depends on whether **n** is positive or negative. For a positive **n**, the value is the same as **n >> s**.

If **n** is negative, the value depends on the type of **n**. If **n** is an **int**, the value is **(n>>s)+(2<<~s)**. If **n** is a **long**, the value is **(n>>s)+(2L<<~s)**.

Assignment Operators

There are twelve assignment operators:

```
=    +=   -=   *=   /=   %=   <<=   >>=   >>>=   &=   ^=   |=
```

Assignment operators take two operands whose type must be of an integral primitive. The left-hand operand must be a variable. For instance:

```
int x = 5;
```

Except for the assignment operator =, the rest work the same way and you should see each of them as consisting of two operators. For example, += is actually + and =. The assignment operator <<= has two operators, << and =.

The two-part assignment operators work by applying the first operator to both operands and then assign the result to the left-hand operand. For example x += 5 is the same as x = x + 5.

x -= 5 is the same as x = x - 5.

x <<= 5 is equivalent to x = x << 5.

x &= 5 produces the same result as x = x &= 5.

Integer Bitwise Operators & | ^

The bitwise operators **&** | **^** perform a bit to bit operation on two operands whose types must be convertible to **int**. **&** indicates an AND operation, | an OR operation, and ^ an exclusive OR operation. For example,

```
0xFFFF & 0x0000 = 0x0000
0xF0F0 & 0xFFFF = 0xF0F0
0xFFFF | 0x000F = 0xFFFF
0xFFF0 ^ 0x00FF = 0xFF0F
```

Logical Operators & | ^

The logical operators **&** | **^** perform a logical operation on two operands that are convertible to **boolean**. **&** indicates an AND operation, | an OR operation, and ^ an exclusive OR operation. For example,

```
true & true  = true
true & false = false
true | false = true
false | false = false
true ^ true = false
false ^ false = false
false ^ true = true
```

Operator Precedence

In most programs, multiple operators often appear in an expression, such as.

```
int a = 1;
int b = 2;
int c = 3;
int d = a + b * c;
```

What is the value of **d** after the code is executed? If you say 9, you're wrong. It's actually 7.

Multiplication operator * takes precedence over addition operator +. As a result, multiplication will be performed before addition. However, if you want the addition to be executed first, you can use parentheses.

```
int d = (a + b) * c;
```

The latter will assign 9 to **d**.

Table 2.4 lists all the operators in the order of precedence. Operators in the same column have equal precedence.

Operator	
postfix operators	[ ] . (params) expr++ expr--
unary operators	++expr --expr +expr -expr ~ !
creation or cast	new (type)expr
multiplicative	* / %
additive	+ -
shift	<< >> >>>
relational	< > <= >=
equality	== !=
bitwise AND	&
bitwise exclusive OR	^
bitwise inclusive OR	|
logical AND	&&
logical OR	||
conditional	? :
assignment	= += -= *= /= %= &= ^= |= <<= >>= >>>=

Table 2.4: The precedence of operators

Note that parentheses have the highest precedence. Parentheses can also make expressions clearer. For example, consider the following code:

```
int x = 5;
int y = 5;
boolean z = x * 5 == y + 20;
```

The value of **z** after comparison is **true**. However, the expression is far from clear.

You can rewrite the last line using parentheses.

```
bool z = (x * 5) == (y + 20);
```

which does not change the result because * and + have higher precedence than ==, but this makes the expression much clearer.

Promotion

Some unary operators (such as +, -, and ~) and binary operators (such as +, -, *, /) cause automatic promotion, i.e. elevation to a wider type such as from **byte** to **int**. Consider the following code:

```
sbyte x = 5;
sbyte y = -x; // error
```

The second line surprisingly causes an error even though a sbyte can accommodate -5. The reason for this is the unary operator - causes the result of **-x** to be promoted to **int**. To rectify the problem, either change **y** to **int** or perform an explicit narrowing conversion like this.

```
sbyte x = 5;
sbyte y = (sbyte) -x;
```

For unary operators, if the type of the operand is **byte**, **sbyte, short**, or **char**, the outcome is promoted to **int**.

For binary operators, the promotion rules are as follows.

- If any of the operands is of type **byte**, **sbyte**, or **short**, then both operands will be converted to **int** and the outcome will be an **int**.
- If any of the operands is of type **double**, then the other operand is converted to **double** and the outcome will be a **double**.

- If any of the operands is of type **float**, then the other operand is converted to **float** and the outcome will be a **float**.
- If any of the operands is of type **long**, then the other operand is converted to **long** and the outcome will be a **long**.

For example, the following code causes a compile error:

```
short x = 200;
short y = 400;
short z = x + y;
```

You can fix this by changing **z** to **int** or perform an explicit narrowing conversion of **x + y**, such as

```
short z = (short) (x + y);
```

Note that the parentheses around **x + y** is required, otherwise only **x** would be converted to **int** and the result of addition of a **short** and an **int** will be an **int**.

Comments

It is good practice to write comments throughout your code, sufficiently explaining what functionality a class provides, what a method does, what a field contains, and so forth.

There are two types of comments in C#, both with syntax similar to comments in C and C++.

- Traditional comments. Enclose a traditional comment in /* and */.
- End-of-line comments. Use double slashes (//) which causes the rest of the line after // to be ignored by the compiler.

For example, here is a comment that describes a method

```
/*
  toUpperCase capitalizes the characters of in a String object
*/
public void toUpperCase(String s) {
```

Here is an end-of-line comment:

```
public int rowCount; //the number of rows from the database
```

Traditional comments do not nest, which means

```
/*
  /* comment 1 */
  comment 2 */
```

is invalid because the first */ after the first /* will terminate the comment. As such, the comment above will have the extra **comment 2 */**, which will generate a compiler error.

On the other hand, end-of-line comments can contain anything, including the sequences of characters /* and */, such as this:

```
// /* this comment is okay */
```

Summary

This chapter presents C# language fundamentals, the basic concepts and topics that you should master before proceeding to more advanced subjects. Topics of discussion include character sets, variables, primitives, literals, operators, operator precedence, and comments.

Chapter 3 continues with statements, another important topic of the C# language.

Chapter 3
Statements

A computer program is a compilation of instructions called statements. There are many types of statements in C# and some—such as **if**, **while**, **for**, and **switch**—are conditional statements that determine the flow of the program. This chapter discusses C# statements, starting with an overview and then providing details of each of them. The **return** statement, which is the statement to exit a method, is discussed in Chapter 4, "Objects and Classes."

An Overview of C# Statements

In programming, a statement is an instruction to do something. Statements control the sequence of execution of a program. Assigning a value to a variable is an example of a statement.

```
x = z + 5;
```

Even a variable declaration is a statement.

```
long secondsElapsed;
```

By contrast, an *expression* is a combination of operators and operands that gets evaluated. For example, **z + 5** is an expression.

In C# a statement is terminated with a semicolon and multiple statements can be written in a single line.

```
x = y + 1; z = y + 2;
```

However, writing multiple statements in a single line is not recommended as it obscures code readability.

Note

In C#, an empty statement is legal and does nothing:

```
;
```

Some expressions can be made statements by terminating them with a semicolon. For example, **x++** is an expression. However, this is a statement:

```
x++;
```

Statements can be grouped in a block. By definition, a block is a sequence of the following programming elements within braces:

- statements
- local class declarations
- local variable declaration statements

A statement and a statement block can be labeled. Label names follow the same rule as C# identifiers and are terminated with a colon. For example, the following statement is labeled **sectionA**.

```
sectionA: x = y + 1;
```

And, here is an example of labeling a block:

```
start:
{
    // statements
}
```

The purpose of labeling a statement or a block is so that it can be referenced by a **goto** statement. Using **goto** is often considered bad practice and is not discussed in this book.

The if Statement

The **if** statement is a conditional branch statement. The syntax of the **if** statement is either one of these two:

```
if (booleanExpression)
{
    statement(s)
```

```
}

if (booleanExpression)
{
    statement(s)
}
else
{
    statement(s)
}
```

If *booleanExpression* evaluates to **true**, the statements in the block following the **if** statement are executed. If it evaluates to **false**, the statements in the **if** block are not executed. If *booleanExpression* evaluates to **false** and there is an **else** block, the statements in the **else** block are executed.

For example, in the following **if** statement, the **if** block will be executed if **x** is greater than 4.

```
if (x > 4)
{
    // statements
}
```

In the following example, the **if** block will be executed if **a** is greater than 3. Otherwise, the **else** block will be executed.

```
if (a > 3)
{
    // statements
}
else
{
    // statements
}
```

Note that the good coding style suggests that statements in a block be indented.

If you are evaluating a **bool** in your **if** statement, it's not necessary to use the == operator like this:

```
bool fileExist = ...
```

```
if (fileExist == true)
```

Instead, you can simply write

```
if (fileExists)
```

By the same token, instead of writing

```
if (fileExists == false)
```

write

```
if (!fileExists)
```

If the expression to be evaluated is too long to be written in a single line, it is recommended that you use two units of indentation for subsequent lines. For example.

```
if (numberOfLoginAttempts < numberOfMaximumLoginAttempts
        || numberOfMinimumLoginAttempts > y)
{
    y++;
}
```

If there is only one statement in an **if** or **else** block, the braces are optional.

```
if (a > 3)
    a++;
else
    a = 3;
```

However, this may pose what is called the dangling else problem. Consider the following example. (Note that **System.Console.WriteLine** is C# code for printing a string or a value.)

```
if (a > 0 || b < 5)
    if (a > 2)
        System.Console.WriteLine("a > 2");
    else
        System.Console.WriteLine("a < 2");
```

The **else** statement is dangling because it is not clear which **if** statement the **else** statement is associated with. An **else** statement is always associated with the immediately preceding **if**. Using braces makes your code clearer.

```
if (a > 0 || b < 5)
{
```

```
    if (a > 2)
    {
        System.Console.WriteLine("a > 2");
    }
    else
    {
        System.Console.WriteLine("a < 2");
    }
}
```

If there are multiple selections, you can also use **if** with a series of **else** statements.

```
if (booleanExpression1)
{
    // statements
}
else if (booleanExpression2)
{
    // statements
}
...
else
{
    // statements
}
```

For example

```
if (a == 1)
{
    System.Console.WriteLine("one");
}
else if (a == 2)
{
    System.Console.WriteLine("two");
}
else if (a == 3)
{
    System.Console.WriteLine("three");
}
else
{
    System.Console.WriteLine("invalid");
}
```

In this case, the **else** statements that are immediately followed by an **if** do not use braces. See also the discussion of the **switch** statement in the section, "The switch Statement" later in this chapter.

The while Statement

In many occasions, you may want to perform an action several times in a row. In other words, you have a block of code that you want executed repeatedly. Intuitively, this can be done by repeating the lines of code. For instance, a beep can be achieved using this line of code:[1]

```
System.Console.Beep();
```

And, to wait for half a second you use this statement.

```
System.Threading.Thread.Sleep(500);
```

Therefore, to produce three beeps with a 500 milliseconds interval between two beeps, you can simply repeat the same code:

```
System.Console.Beep();
System.Threading.Thread.Sleep(500);
System.Console.Beep();
System.Threading.Thread.Sleep(500);
System.Console.Beep();
```

However, there are circumstances where repeating code does not work. Here are some of those:

- The number of repetition is higher than 5, which means the number of lines of code increases five fold. If there is a line that you need to fix in the block, copies of the same line must also be modified.
- If the number of repetitions is not known in advance.

A much cleverer way is to put the repeated code in a loop. This way, you only write the code once but you can instruct C# to execute the code any number of times. One way to create a loop is by using the **while** statement,

---

[1] What this line of code and the following lines of code do will become clear after you read Chapter 4.

which is the topic of discussion of this section. Another way is to use the **for** statement, which is explained in the next section.

The **while** statement has the following syntax.

```
while (booleanExpression)
{
    statement(s)
}
```

Here, *statement(s)* will be executed as long as *booleanExpression* evaluates to **true**. If there is only a single statement inside the braces, you may omit the braces. For clarity, however, you should always use braces even when there is only one statement.

As an example of the **while** statement, the following code prints integer numbers that are less than three.

```
int i = 0;
while (i < 3)
{
    System.Console.WriteLine(i);
    i++;
}
```

Note that the execution of the code in the loop is dependent on the value of **i**, which is incremented with each iteration until it reaches 3.

To produce three beeps with an interval of 500 milliseconds, use this code:

```
int j = 0;
while (j < 3) {
    System.Console.Beep();
    try
    {
        Thread.currentThread().sleep(500);
    }
    catch (Exception e)
    {
    }
    j++;
}
```

Sometimes, you use an expression that always evaluates to **true** (such as the boolean literal **true**) but relies on the **break** statement to escape from the loop.

```
int k = 0;
while (true)
{
    System.Console.WriteLine(k);
    k++;
    if (k > 2) {
        break;
    }
}
```

You will learn about the **break** statement in the section, "The break Statement" later in this chapter.

The do-while Statement

The **do-while** statement is like the **while** statement, except that the associated block always gets executed at least once. Its syntax is as follows:

```
do
{
    statement(s)
} while (booleanExpression);
```

With **do-while**, you put the statement(s) to be executed after the **do** keyword. Just like the **while** statement, you can omit the braces if there is only one statement within them. However, always use braces for the sake of clarity.

For example, here is an example of the **do-while** statement:

```
int i = 0;
do
{
    System.Console.WriteLine(i);
    i++;
} while (i < 3);
```

This prints the following to the console:

```
0
1
2
```

The following **do-while** demonstrates that at least the code in the **do** block will be executed once even though the initial value of **j** used to test the expression **j < 3** evaluates to **false**.

```
int j = 4;
do
{
    System.Console.WriteLine(j);
    j++;
} while (j < 3);
```

This prints the following on the console.

```
4
```

The for Statement

The **for** statement is like the **while** statement, i.e. you use it to enclose code that needs to be executed multiple times. However, **for** is more complex than **while**.

The **for** statement starts with an initialization, followed by an expression evaluation for each iteration and the execution of a statement block if the expression evaluates to **true**. An update statement will also be executed after the execution of the statement block for each iteration.

The **for** statement has following syntax:

```
for ( init ; booleanExpression ; update ) {
    statement(s)
}
```

Here, *init* is an initialization that will be performed before the first iteration, *booleanExpression* is a boolean expression which will cause the execution of *statement(s)* if it evaluates to **true**, and *update* is a statement that will be executed *after* the execution of the statement block. *init*, *expression*, and *update* are optional.

The **for** statement will stop only if one of the following conditions is met:

- *booleanEpression* evaluates to **false**
- A **break** or **continue** statement is executed
- A runtime error occurs.

It is common to declare a variable and assign a value to it in the initialization part. The variable declared will be visible to the *expression* and *update* parts as well as to the statement block.

For example, the following **for** statement loops five times and each time prints the value of **i**.

```
for (int i = 0; i < 3; i++)
{
    System.Console.WriteLine(i);
}
```

The **for** statement starts by declaring an **int** named **i** and assigning 0 to it:

```
int i = 0;
```

It then evaluates the expression **i < 3**, which evaluates to **true** since **i** equals 0. As a result, the statement block is executed, and the value of **i** is printed. It then performs the update statement **i++**, which increments **i** to 1. That concludes the first loop.

The **for** statement then evaluates the value of **i < 3** again. The result is again **true** because **i** equals 1. This causes the statement block to be executed and **1** is printed on the console. After that, the update statement **i++** is executed, incrementing **i** to 2. That concludes the second loop.

Next, the expression **i < 3** is evaluated and the result is **true** because **i** equals 2. This causes the statement block to be run and 2 is printed on the console. Afterwards, the update statement **i++** is executed, causing **i** to be equal to 3. This concludes the second loop.

Finally, the expression **i < 3** is evaluated again, and the result is **false**. This stops the **for** loop.

This is what you will see on the console:

```
0
```

```
1
2
```

Note that the variable **i** is not visible anywhere else since it is declared within the **for** loop.

Note also that if the statement block within **for** only consists of one statement, you can remove the braces, so in this case the above **for** statement can be rewritten as:

```
for (int i = 0; i < 3; i++)
    System.Console.WriteLine(i);
```

However, using braces even if there is only one statement makes your code clearer.

Here is another example of the **for** statement.

```
for (int i = 0; i < 3; i++)
{
    if (i % 2 == 0)
    {
        System.Console.WriteLine(i);
    }
}
```

This one loops three times. For each iteration the value of **i** is tested. If **i** is even, its value is printed. The result of the **for** loop is as follows:

```
0
2
```

The following **for** loop is similar to the previous case, but uses **i += 2** as the update statement. As a result, it only loops twice, when **i** equals 0 and when it is 2.

```
for (int i = 0; i < 3; i += 2)
{
    System.Console.WriteLine(i);
}
```

The result is

```
0
2
```

A statement that decrements a variable is often used too. Consider the following **for** loop:

```
for (int i = 3; i > 0; i--)
{
    System.Console.WriteLine(i);
}
```

which prints:

```
3
2
1
```

The initialization part of the **for** statement is optional. In the following **for** loop, the variable **j** is declared outside the loop, so potentially **j** can be used from other points in the code outside the **for** statement block.

```
int j = 0;
for ( ; j < 3; j++) {
    System.Console.WriteLine(j);
}
// j is visible here
```

As mentioned previously, the update statement is optional. The following **for** statement moves the update statement to the end of the statement block. The result is the same.

```
int k = 0;
for ( ; k < 3; )
{
    System.Console.WriteLine(k);
    k++;
}
```

In theory, you can even omit the *booleanExpression* part. For example, the following **for** statement does not have one, and the loop is only terminated with the **break** statement. See the section, "The break Statement" for more information.

```
int m = 0;
for ( ; ; )
{
    System.Console.WriteLine(m);
    m++;
```

```
      if (m > 4)
      {
          break;
      }
}
```

If you compare **for** and **while**, you'll see that you can always replace the **while** statement with **for**. This is to say that

```
while (expression)
{
    ...
}
```

can always be written as

```
for ( ; expression; )
{
    ...
}
```

> **Note**
> In addition, **foreach** can iterate over an array or a collection. See Chapters 5, "Core Classes" and Chapter 13, "Collections" for the discussions of **foreach**.

The break Statement

The **break** statement is used to break from an enclosing **do**, **while**, **for**, or **switch** statement. It is a compile error to use **break** anywhere else.

For example, consider the following code

```
int i = 0;
while (true)
{
    System.Console.WriteLine(i);
    i++;
    if (i > 3) {
        break;
    }
}
```

The result is

```
0
1
2
3
```

Note that **break** breaks the loop without executing the rest of the statements in the block.

Here is another example of break, this time in a **for** loop.

```
int m = 0;
for ( ; ; )
{
    System.Console.WriteLine(m);
    m++;
    if (m > 4) {
        break;
    }
}
```

The continue Statement

The **continue** statement is like **break** but it only stops the execution of the current iteration and causes control to begin with the next iteration.

For example, the following code prints the number 0 to 9, except 5.

```
for (int i = 0; i < 10; i++)
{
    if (i == 5) {
        continue;
    }
    System.Console.WriteLine(i);
}
```

When **i** is equals to 5, the expression of the **if** statement evaluates to **true** and causes the **continue** statement to be called. As a result, the statement below it that prints the value of **i** is not executed and control continues with the next loop, i.e. for **i** equal to 6.

The switch Statement

An alternative to a series of **else if**, as discussed in the last part of the section, "The if Statement," is the **switch** statement. **switch** allows you to choose a block of statements to run from a selection of code, based on the return value of an expression. The expression used in the **switch** statement must return an **int**, a **String**, or an enumerated value.

Note

The **String** class is discussed in Chapter 5, "Core Classes" and enumerated values in Chapter 10, "Enums."

The syntax of the **switch** statement is as follows.

```
switch(expression)
{
    case value_1 :
        [statement(s);]
        [break | goto label;]
    case value_2 :
        [statement(s);]
        [break | goto label;]
        .
        .
        .
    case value_n :
        [statement(s);]
        [break | goto label;]
    default:
        [statement(s);]
        [break | goto label;]
}
```

After each statements in a switch case, you can either break or jump to a label using **goto**. The statements and jump statement are optional.

Here is an example of the **switch** statement. If the value of **i** is 1, "One player is playing this game." is printed. If the value is 2, "Two players are playing this game is printed." If the value is 3, "Three players are playing this game is printed. For any other value, "You did not enter a valid value." will be printed.

```
int i = ...;
switch (i)
{
    case 1 :
        System.Console.WriteLine(
                "One player is playing this game.");
        break;
    case 2 :
        System.Console.WriteLine(
                "Two players are playing this game.");
        break;
    case 3 :
        System.Console.WriteLine(
                "Three players are playing this game.");
        break;
    default:
        System.Console.WriteLine(
                "You did not enter a valid value.");
        break;
}
```

Summary

The sequence of execution of a C# program is controlled by statements. In this chapter, you have learned the following control statements: **if**, **while**, **do-while**, **for**, **break**, **continue**, and **switch**. Understanding how to use these statements is crucial to writing correct programs.

Chapter 4
Objects and Classes

This chapter introduces you to objects and classes. If you are new to OOP, you may want to read this chapter carefully because a good understanding of OOP is key to writing quality programs.

This chapter starts by explaining what an object is and what constitutes a class. It then teaches you how to create objects in C# using the **new** keyword, how objects are stored in memory, how classes can be organized into namespaces, how to use access control to achieve encapsulation, and how C# manages unused objects. In addition, method overloading and static class members are explained.

What Is a C# Object?

When developing an application in an OOP language, you create a model that resembles a real-life situation to solve your problem. Take for example a company payroll application, which can calculate the take home pay of an employee and the amount of income tax payable. Such an application would have a **Company** object to represent the company using the application, **Employee** objects that represent the employees working for the company, **Tax** objects to represent the tax details of each employee, and so on. Before you can start programming such applications, however, you need to understand what C# objects are and how to create them.

Let's begin with a look at objects in life. Objects are everywhere, living (persons, pets, etc) and otherwise (cars, houses, streets, etc); concrete (books, televisions, etc) and abstract (love, knowledge, tax rate, regulations, and so forth). Every object has two features: attributes and actions. For example, the following are some of a car's attributes:

- color
- number of tires
- plate number

Additionally, a car can perform these actions:

- run
- brake

As another example, a dog has the following attributes: color, age, type, weight, and so on. And it also can bark, run, urinate, sniff, etc.

A C# object also has attribute(s) and can perform action(s). In C#, attributes are called fields and actions are called methods. In other programming languages fields and methods may be called other names. For example, methods are often called functions.

Both fields and methods are optional, meaning some C# objects may not have fields but have methods and some others may have fields but not methods. Some, of course, have both attributes and methods and some have neither.

How do you create an object in C#? To create an object, you need a class, a blueprint for the object. Classes are explained in the next section.

C# Classes

A class is a blueprint or a template for creating objects of identical type. If you have an **Employee** class, you can create any number of **Employee** objects. To create **Street** objects, you need a **Street** class. A class determines what kind of objects you get. For example, if you create an **Employee** class that has **Age** and **Position** fields, all **Employee** objects created out of this **Employee** class will have **Age** and **Position** fields as well. No more no less. The class determines the objects.

In summary, classes are an OOP tool that enable programmers to create the abstraction of a problem. In OOP, abstraction is the act of using programming objects to represent real-world objects. As such, programming objects do not need to have the details of real-world objects. For instance, if an **Employee** object in a payroll application needs only be able to work and receive a salary, then the **Employee** class needs only two methods, **Work** and **ReceiveSalary**. OOP abstraction ignores the fact that a real-world employee can do many other things including eat, run, kiss, and kick.

Classes are the fundamental building blocks of a C# program. A C# beginner needs to consider three things when writing a class:

- the class name
- the fields
- the methods

There are other things that can be present in a class, but they will be discussed later.

A class declaration must use the keyword **class** followed by a class name. Also, a class has a body within braces. Here is the general syntax for classes:

```
class className
{
    [class body]
}
```

For example, Listing 4.1 shows a C# class named **Employee**, where the lines in bold are the class body.

Listing 4.1: The Employee class

```
class Employee
{
    int Age;
    double Salary;
}
```

Note

By convention, class names capitalize the initial of each word. For example, here are some names that follow this convention: **Employee, Boss, DateUtility, PostOffice, RegularRateCalculator**. This type of naming convention is known as Pascal naming convention. The other convention, the camel naming convention, capitalize the initial of each word, except the first word, e.g. **postOffice, dateUtility, crayon**.

A class definition in C# must be saved in a file with .cs extension. The file name does not have to be the same as the class name.

Note

To visualize models in an object-oriented program, software engineers often use standard notations defined in Unified Modeling Language (UML). In UML class diagrams, a class is represented by a rectangle that consists of three parts: the topmost part is the class name, the middle part is the list of fields, and the bottom part is the list of methods. (See Figure 4.1) The fields and methods can be hidden if showing them is not important.

Figure 4.1: The Employee class in the UML class diagram

Fields

Fields are variables. They can be value types or references to objects. For example, the **Employee** class in Listing 4.1 has two fields, **Age** and **Salary**, which are likely of value type. However, a field can also refer to an object. For instance, an **Empoyee** class may have an **Address** field of type **Address**, which is a class that represents a street address:

```
Address address;
```

In other words, an object can contain other objects, that is if the class of the former contains variables that reference to the latter.

Field names should follow Pascal naming convention. The initial of each word in the field is written with a capital letter. For example, here are some "good" field names: **Age**, **MaxAge**, **Address**, **ValidAddress**, **NumberOfRows**.

Methods

Methods define actions that a class's objects (or instances) can do. A method has a declaration part and a body. The declaration part consists of a return value, the method name, and a list of arguments. The body contains code that performs the action.

To declare a method, use the following syntax:

```
returnType methodName (listOfArguments)
```

The return type of a method can be an intrinsic data type, an object, or void. The **void** return type means that the method returns nothing. The declaration part of a method is also called the signature of the method.

For example, here is the **GetSalary** method that returns a **double**.

```
double GetSalary()
```

The **GetSalary** method does not take arguments.

As another example, here is a method that returns an **Address** object.

```
Address GetAddress()
```

And, here is a method that accepts an argument:

```
int Negate(int number)
```

If a method takes more than one argument, two arguments are separated by a comma. For example, the following **Add** method takes two **int**s and return an **int**.

```
int Add(int a, int b)
```

The Method Main

A special method called **Main** provides the entry point to an application. An application normally has many classes and only one of the classes needs to have a **Main** method. This method allows the class containing it to be invoked.

In C# the return value of **Main** can be **void** or **int**. It also may accept a **string[]** argument. The following are valid **Main** methods, only one of them needs to be present in your application.

The signature of the **Main** method is as follows.

```
static void Main()

static void Main(string[] args)

static int Main()

static int Main(string[] args)
```

If you wonder why there is the word "static" before **Main**, you will get the answer towards the end of this chapter.

If your **Main** method accepts arguments, you can pass arguments to it when running the class. To pass arguments, type them after the executable name. Two arguments are separated by a space.

```
MyApp arg1 arg2 arg3
```

All arguments must be passed as strings. For instance, to pass two arguments, "1" and "safeMode" when running the **Counter** class, you would type this:

```
Counter 1 safeMode
```

To pass line arguments to the **Main** method in Visual C# 2010 Express, right-click your project name in Solution Explorer and click **Properties**, then select **Debug** in the Properties pane. You will see the Debug pane like the one in Figure 4.2. Enter your argument(s) in the Command line arguments box and save the arguments by pressing **Ctrl+S**.

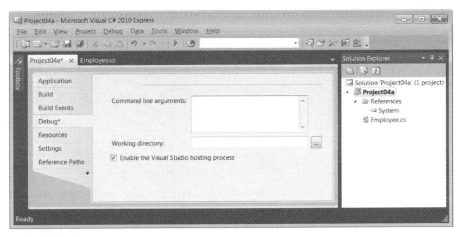

Figure 4.2: Passing line arguments in Visual C# 2010 Express

Constructors

Every class must have at least one constructor. Otherwise, no objects could be created out of the class and the class would be useless. As such, if your class does not explicitly define a constructor, the compiler adds one for you.

A constructor is used to construct an object. A constructor looks like a method and is sometimes called a constructor method. However, unlike a method, a constructor does not have a return value, not even **void**. Additionally, a constructor must have the same name as the class.

The syntax for a constructor is as follows.

```
constructorName (listOfArguments)
{
    [constructor body]
}
```

A constructor may have zero argument, in which case it is called a no-argument (or no-arg, for short) constructor. Constructor arguments can be used to initialize the fields in the object.

If the C# compiler adds a no-arg constructor to a class because the class has none, the addition will be implicit, i.e. it will not be displayed in the source file. However, if there is a constructor, regardless of the number of arguments it accepts, no constructor will be added to the class by the compiler.

You can have multiple constructors in your class as long as each has a different set of arguments. As an example, Listing 4.2 adds two constructors to the **Employee** class in Listing 4.1.

Listing 4.2: The Employee class with constructors

```
public class Employee
{
    public int Age;
    public double Salary;
    public Employee() {

    }

    public Employee(int AgeValue, double SalaryValue) {
        Age = AgeValue;
        Salary = SalaryValue;
    }
}
```

The second constructor is particularly useful. Without it, to assign values to age and position, you would need to write extra lines of code to initialize the fields:

```
Employee employee = new Employee();
employee.Age = 20;
employee.Salary = 90000.00;
```

With the second constructor, you can pass the values at the same time you create an object.

```
new Employee(20, 90000.00);
```

The **new** keyword is new to you, but you will learn how to use it in the next section.

Class Members in the UML Class Diagram

Figure 4.3 depicts a class in a UML class diagram. The diagram provides a quick summary of all fields and methods. UML allows you to include field types and method signatures. For example, Figure 4.3 presents a **Book** class with five fields and one method.

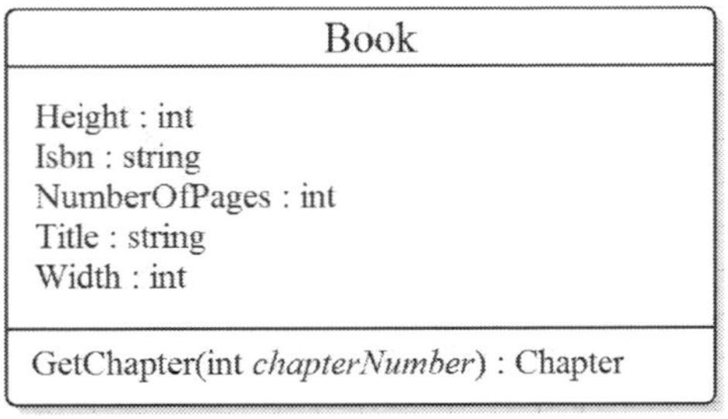

Book
Height : int Isbn : string NumberOfPages : int Title : string Width : int
GetChapter(int *chapterNumber*) : Chapter

Figure 4.3: Including class member information in a class diagram

Note that in a UML class diagram a field and its type is separated by a colon. A method's argument list is presented in parentheses and its return type is written after a colon.

Creating Objects

Now that you know how to write a class, it is time to learn how to create an object from a class. An object is also called an instance. The word construct is often used in lieu of create, thus constructing an **Employee** object. Another term commonly used is *instantiate*. Instantiating the **Employee** class is the same as creating an instance of **Employee**.

There are a number of ways to create an object, but the most common one is by using the **new** keyword. **new** is always followed by the constructor of the class to be instantiated. For example, to create an **Employee** object, you would write:

```
new Employee();
```

Most of the time, you will want to assign the created object to an object variable (or a reference variable), so that you can manipulate the object later. To achieve this, you just need to declare an object reference with the same type as the object. For instance:

```
Employee employee = new Employee();
```

Here, **employee** is an object reference of type **Employee**.

Once you have an object, you can call its methods and access its fields, by using the object reference that was assigned the object. You use a period (.) to call a method or a field. For example:

```
objectReference.MethodName
objectReference.FieldName
```

The following code, for instance, creates an **Employee** object and assigns values to its **Age** and **Salary** fields:

```
Employee employee = new Employee();
employee.Age = 24;
employee.Salary = 50000;
```

When an object is created, the CLR also performs initialization that assigns default values to fields.

Note that you never have to explicitly destroy your objects to free up memory. The garbage collector inside the CLR takes care of it. This, however, does not entail that you can create as many objects as you want because memory is (still) limited and it takes some time for the garbage collector to start. That's right, you can still run out of memory.

The null Keyword

A reference variable refers to an object. There are times, however, when a reference variable does not have a value (the variable is not referencing an object). Such a reference variable is said to have a null value. For example, the following class level reference variable is of type **Book** but has not been assigned a value;

```
Book book; // book is null
```

If you declare a local reference variable within a method but do not assign an object to it and later try to use it, you will need to assign null to it to stop the compiler's whining:

```
Book book = null;
```

Class-level reference variables will be initialized when an instance is created, therefore you do not need to assign **null** to them.

Trying to access the field or method of a null variable reference raises an error, such as in the following code:

```
Book book = null;
Console.WriteLine(book.title); // error because book is null
```

You can test if a reference variable is **null** by using the == operator. For instance.

```
if (book == null)
{
    book = new Book();
}
Console.WriteLine(book.title);
```

Objects in Memory

When you declare a variable in your class, either in the class level or in the method level, you allocate memory space for data that will be assigned to the variable. For value types, it is easy to calculate the amount of memory taken. For example, declaring an **int** costs you four bytes and declaring a **long** sets you back eight bytes. However, calculation for reference variables is different.

When a program runs, some memory space is allocated for data. This data space is logically divided into two, the stack and the heap. Value types are allocated in the stack and objects reside in the heap.

When you declare a value type, a few bytes are allocated in the stack. When you declare a reference variable, some bytes are also set aside in the stack, but the memory does not contain an object's data, it contains the address of the object in the heap. In other words, when you declare

```
Book book;
```

some bytes are set aside for the reference variable **book**. The initial value of **book** is **null** because there is not yet object assigned to it. When you write

```
Book book = new Book();
```

you create an instance of **Book**, which is stored in the heap, and assign the address of the instance to the reference variable **book**. A C# reference variable is like a C++ pointer except that you cannot manipulate a reference variable. In C#, a reference variable is used to access the member of the object it is referring to. Therefore, if the **Book** class has a public method named **Review**, you can call the method by using this syntax:

```
book.Review();
```

An object can be referenced by more than one reference variable. For example,

```
Book myBook = new Book();
Book yourBook = myBook;
```

The second line copies the value of **myBook** to **yourBook**. As a result, **yourBook** is now referencing the same **Book** object as **myBook**.

Figure 4.4 illustrates memory allocation for a **Book** object referenced by **myBook** and **yourBook**.

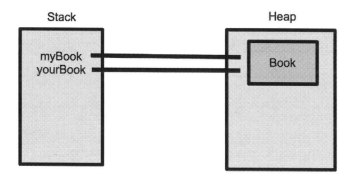

Figure 4.4: An object referenced by two variables

On the other hand, the following code creates two different **Book** objects:

```
Book myBook = new Book();
Book yourBook = new Book();
```

The memory allocation for this code is illustrated in Figure 4.5.

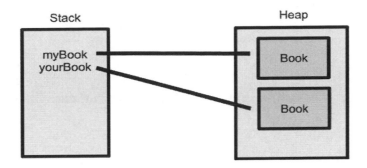

Figure 4.5: Two objects referenced by two variables

Now, how about an object that contains another object? For example, consider the code in Listing 4.3 that shows an **Employee** class that contains an **Address** class.

Listing 4.3: The Employee class that contains another class

```
public class Employee
{
    Address address = new Address();
}
```

When you create an **Employee** object using the following code, an **Address** object is also created.

```
Employee employee = new Employee();
```

Figure 4.6 depicts the position of each object in the heap.

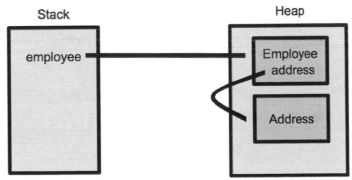

Figure 4.6: An object "within" another object

It turns out that the **Address** object is not really inside the **Employee** object. However, the **address** reference variable in the **Employee** object references the **Address** object, thus allowing the **Employee** object to manipulate the **Address** object. Because in C# there is no way of accessing an object except through a reference variable assigned the object's address, no one else can access the **Address** object 'within' the **Employee** object.

C# Namespaces

Namespaces allow you to organize your classes and other types to create a truly unique name for your type and avoid naming conflicts. A namespace may contain any number of classes and other types and even another namespace. Here is a class that is declared within a namespace.

```
namespace MyNamespace
{
    class MyClass
    {

    }
}
```

If you do not declare your class in a namespace, the C# compiler adds a default one for you, the global namespace.

It is possible to define a namespace in multiple declarations, such as the following:

```
namespace YourNamespace
{
    class Class1
    {

    }
}

namespace YourNamespace
{
    class Class2
    {

    }
```

```
}
```

The .NET Framework also uses namespaces to organize its class library. For example, the **Console** class that you've been using to print a string belongs to the **System** namespace.

To use types in a namespace, you use the **using** directive at the beginning of your file. For instance, if you declare

```
using System;
```

you'll be able to use members of the **System** namespace in your code. Therefore, you can simply write

```
Console.WriteLine("Program terminated.);
```

If you don't import **System**, you will have to include the fully-qualified name of the class you use, e.g.

```
System.Console.WriteLine("Program terminated.);
```

Encapsulation and Class Access Control

An OOP principle, encapsulation is a mechanism that protects parts of an object that need to be secure and exposes only parts that are safe to be exposed. The television is a good example of encapsulation. Inside it are thousands of electronic components that together form the parts that can receive signals and decode them into images and sound. These components are not to be exposed to users, however, so Sony and other manufacturers wrap them in a strong metallic or plastic cover that does not break easily. For a television to be easy to use, it exposes buttons that the user can touch to turn on and off the set, adjust brightness, turn up and down the volume, and so on.

Back to encapsulation in OOP, let's take as an example a class that can encode and decode messages. The class exposes two methods called **Encode** and **Decode**, which users of the class can access. Internally, there are dozens of variables used to store temporary values and other methods that perform supporting tasks. The author of the class hides these variables and other methods because allowing access to them may compromise the security of the encoding/decoding algorithms. Besides, exposing too many things makes the class harder to use. As you can see later, encapsulation is a powerful feature.

C# supports encapsulation through access control. Access control is governed by access control modifiers, or simply called access modifiers for brevity. There are four access modifiers in C#: **public**, **protected**, **internal**, and **private**.

Access control modifiers can be applied to classes or class members. A class can be either public or internal. A class by default have **internal** accessibility unless it is explicitly declared as **public**. Public classes can be accessed by other types in any namespace. By contrast, an internal class is only accessible to other types in the same namespace. A class without an access modifier has an internal access level.

For example, **ClassA** in the following snippet is a public class.

```
namespace CompanyA
{
    public class ClassA
    {

    }
}
```

ClassA can be accessed by any type within the **CompanyA** namespace as well as by other types outside the namespace. On the other hand, the following **ClassB** and **ClassC** classes only accessible to other types in the **CompanyA** namespace. This is because both **ClassB** and **ClassC** have internal accessibility.

```
namespace CompanyA
{
    internal class ClassB
    {

    }

    class ClassC
    {

    }
}
```

A class in the default namespace can be used from any other classes in any namespace, even though the class is not public. For example, in this snippet the **Book** class can use the **Chapter** class, which is not enclosed in a namespace and is therefore in the default namespace.

```
class Chapter
{

}

namespace MyCompany
{
    class Book
    {
        Chapter chapter = new Chapter();
    }
}
```

On the other hand, this will not compile, because **House** is an internal class of the **YourCompany** namespace and cannot be accessed from a class in another namespace.

```
namespace YourCompany
{
    class House
    {

    }
}

namespace MyCompany
{
    class Person
    {
        House house = new House(); // compile error
    }
}
```

You can turn the **House** class to public and access it from another namespace, like this:

```
namespace YourCompany
{
    public class House
```

```
        {
        }
    }

namespace MyCompany
{
    using YourCompany;
    class Person
    {
        House house = new House(); // compile error
    }
}
```

Note that a namespace does not take a modifier and is always public.

Now let's turn to class members. A class member can have one of these five accessibility levels.

- **public**. Access is not restricted.
- **protected**. Access is limited to the containing class or types derived from the containing class.
- **internal**. Access is limited to the current assembly.
- **protected internal**. Access is limited to the current assembly or types derived from the containing class.
- **private**. Access is limited to the containing type.

A public class member can be accessed by any other classes that can access the class containing the class member. For example, the **ToString** method of the **System.Object** class in the .NET Framework class library is public. Therefore, once you construct an **Object** object, you can call its **ToString** method because **ToString** is public.

```
Object obj = new Object();
obj.ToString();
```

Recall that you access a class member by using this syntax:

referenceVariable.memberName

In the preceding code, **obj** is a reference variable to an instance of **System.Object** and **ToString** is the method defined in the **System.Object** class.

A protected class member has a more restricted access level. It can be accessed only from the containing class or a child class of the containing class. A class's private members can only be accessed from inside the same class.

How about constructors? Access levels to constructors are the same as those for fields and methods. Therefore, constructors can have public, protected, internal, protected internal, and private access levels. You may think that all constructors must be public because the intention of having a constructor is to make the class instantiable. However, to your surprise, this is not so. Some constructors are made private so that their classes cannot be instantiated by using the **new** keyword. Private constructors are normally used in singleton classes. If you are interested in this topic, there are articles on this topic that you can find easily on the Internet.

Note

In a UML class diagram, you can include information on class member access level. Prefix a public member with +, a protected member with # and a private member with -. Members with no prefix are regarded as having the default access level. Figure 4.7 shows the **Manager** class with members having various access levels.

Figure 4.7: Including class member access level in a UML class diagram

The this Keyword

You use the **this** keyword from any method or constructor to refer to the current object. For example, if you have a class-level field having the same name as a local variable, you can use this syntax to refer to the former:

```
this.field
```

A common use is in the constructor that accepts values used to initialize fields. Consider the **Box** class in Listing 4.4.

Listing 4.4: The Box class

```
namespace Project04a
{
    public class Box
    {
        int Length;
        int Width;
        int Height;
        public Box(int length, int width, int height)
        {
            this.Length = length;
            this.Width = width;
            this.Height = height;
        }
    }
}
```

The **Box** class has three fields, **Length**, **Width**, and **Height**. Its constructor accepts three arguments used to initialize the fields. It is very convenient to use **length**, **width**, and **height** as the parameter names because they reflect what they are. Inside the constructor, **length** refers to the **length** argument, not the **length** field. **this.length** refers to the class-level **length** field.

Using Other Classes

It is common to use other classes from the class you are writing. Using classes in the same namespace as your current class is allowed by default.

However, to use classes in another namespace, you must first import the namespace using the keyword **using**. For example, to use the members of the **System** namespace, such as the **System.Console** class, from your code, you must have the following **using** statement:

```
namespace Project04a
{
    using System;
    public class Demo
    {
        public void Test()
        {
            // can use System.Console because we imported System
            Console.WriteLine("Testing ...");
        }
    }
}
```

Note that **using** statements must be inside the namespace but before the class declaration. The **using** keyword can appear multiple times in a namespace.

```
namespace Project04a
{
    using System;
    using System.IO;

}
```

The only way to use classes that belong to other namespaces without importing them is to use the fully qualified names of the classes in your code. For example, the following statement uses **System.Console** without importing **System**.

```
System.Console.Beep();
```

If you are using identically-named classes from different namespaces, you must use the fully qualified names when declaring the classes. For example, in Listing 4.5 the **MyCompany.Person** class uses the **Project1.Chair** and **Project2.Chair** classes. Without fully-qualified names, it is ambiguous which **Chair** class is being used.

Listing 4.5: Using fully qualified names

```
namespace Project1
{
    public class Chair
    {
    }
}

namespace Project2
{
    public class Chair
    {
    }
}

namespace MyCompany
{
    class Person
    {
        static void Main()
        {
            Project1.Chair p1Chair = new Project1.Chair();
            Project2.Chair p2Chair = new Project2.Chair();
        }
    }
}
```

A class that uses another class is said to "depend on" the latter. A UML diagram that depicts this dependency is shown in Figure 4.8.

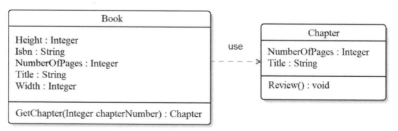

Figure 4.8: Dependency in the UML class diagram

A dependency relationship is represented by a dashed line with an arrow. In Figure 4.8 the **Book** class is dependent on **Chapter** because the **GetChapter** method returns a **Chapter** object.

Static Members

You have learned that to access a public field or method of an object, you use a period after the object reference, such as:

```
// Create an instance of Book
Book book = new Book();
// access the Review method
book.Review();
```

This implies that you must create an object first before you can access its members. However, in previous chapters, there were examples that used **System.Console.WriteLine** to print values to the console. You may have noticed that you could call the **WriteLine** method without first having to construct a **Console** object. How come you did not have to do something like this?

```
Console console = new Console();
console.WriteLine("blah);
```

Rather, you use a period after the class name:

```
Console.WriteLine("blah);
```

C# (and many OOP languages) supports the notion of static members, which are class members that can be called without first instantiating the class. The **WriteLine** method in **System.Console** is static, which explains why you can use it without first instantiating **System.Console**.

Static members are not tied to class instances. Rather, they can be called without having an instance. In fact, the method **Main**, which acts as the entry point to a class, is static because it must be called before any object is created.

To create a static member, you use the keyword **static** in front of a field or method declaration. If there is an access modifier, the **static** keyword may come before or after the access modifier. These two are correct:

```
public static int NumberOfPages;
static public int NumberOfPages;
```

However, the first form is more often used.

For example, Listing 4.6 shows the **MathUtil** class with a static method:

Listing 4.6: The MathUtil class

```
namespace Project04a
{
    class MathUtil
    {
        public static int Add(int a, int b)
        {
            return a + b;
        }
    }
}
```

To use the **Add** method, you can simply call it like this:

```
MathUtil.Add(a, b)
```

The term instance methods/fields are used to refer to non-static methods and fields.

From inside a static method, you cannot call instance methods or instance fields because they only exist after you create an object. You can access other static methods or fields from a static method, however.

A common confusion that a beginner often encounter is when they cannot compile their class because they are calling instance members from the **Main** method. Listing 4.7 shows such a class.

Listing 4.7: Calling non-static members from a static method

```
namespace Project04a
{
    using System;
    public class StaticDemo
    {
        public int B = 8;
        static void Main()
        {
            Console.WriteLine(B);
        }
    }
}
```

The line in bold causes a compile error because it attempts to access non-static field **B** from the **Main** static method. There are two solutions to this.

1. Make **B** static
2. Create an instance of the class, then access **B** by using the object reference.

Which solution is appropriate depends on the situation. It often takes years of OOP experience to come up with a good decision that you're comfortable with.

Note

You can only declare a static variable in a class level. You cannot declare local static variables even if the method is static.

How about static reference variables? You can declare static reference variables. The variable will contain an address, but the object referenced is stored in the heap. For instance

```
static Book book = new Book();
```

Static reference variables provide a good way of exposing the same object that needs to be shared among other different objects.

Note

In UML class diagrams, static members are underlined. For example, Figure 4.9 shows the **MathUtil** class with the static method **Add**.

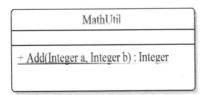

Figure 4.9: Static members in UML class diagrams

Variable Scope

You have seen that you can declare variables in several different places:

- In a class body as class fields. Variables declared here are referred to as class-level variables.
- As parameters of a method or constructor.
- In a method's body or a constructor's body.
- Within a statement block, such as inside a **while** or **for** block.

Now it's time to learn the scope of variables.

Variable scope refers to the accessibility of a variable. The rule is that variables defined in a block are only accessible from within the block. The scope of the variable is the block in which it is defined. For example, consider the following **for** statement.

```
for (int x = 0; x < 5; x++)
{
    System.Console.WriteLine(x);
}
```

The variable **x** is declared within the **for** statement. As a result, **x** is only available from within this **for** block. It is not accessible or visible from anywhere else.

Rule number 2 is a nested block can access variables declared in the outer block. Consider this code.

```
for (int x = 0; x < 5; x++)
{
    for (int y = 0; y < 3; y++)
    {
        System.Console.WriteLine(x);
        System.Console.WriteLine(y);
    }
}
```

The preceding code is valid because the inner **for** block can access **x**, which is declared in the outer **for** block.

Following the rules, variables declared as method parameters can be accessed from within the method body. Also, class-level variables are accessible from anywhere in the class.

If a method declares a local variable that has the same name as a class-level variable, the former will 'shadow' the latter. To access the class-level variable from inside the method body, use the **this** keyword.

Method Overloading

Method names are very important and should reflect what the methods do. In many circumstances, you may want to use the same name for multiple methods because they have similar functionality. For instance, the method **PrintString** may take a **String** argument and prints the string. However, the same class may also provide a method that prints part of a **String** and accepts two arguments, the **String** to be printed and the character position to start printing from. You want to call the latter method **PrintString** too because it does print a **String**, but that would be the same as the first **PrintString** method.

Thankfully, it is okay in C# to have multiple methods having the same name, as long as each method accept different sets of argument types. In other words, in our example, it is legal to have these two methods in the same class.

```
public void PrintString(String string)
public void PrintString(String string, int offset)
```

This feature is called method overloading.

The return value of the method is not taken into consideration. As such, these two methods must not exist in the same class:

```
public int CountRows(int number);
public string countRows(int number);
```

This is because a method can be called without assigning its return value to a variable. In such situations, having the above **CountRows** methods would confuse the compiler as it would not know which method is being called when you write

```
System.Console.Write(countRows(3));.
```

A trickier situation is depicted in the following methods whose signatures are very similar.

```
public int PrintNumber(int i)
{
    return i*2;
}

public long PrintNumber(long l)
{
    return l*3;
}
```

It is legal to have these two methods in the same class. However, you might wonder, which method is being called if you write **PrintNumber(3)**?

The key is to recall from Chapter 2, "Language Fundamentals" that a numeric literal will be translated into an **int** unless it is suffixed **L** or **l**.. Therefore, **printNumber(3)** will invoke this method:

```
public int PrintNumber(int i)
```

To call the second, pass a **long**:

```
printNumber(3L);
```

Note
Static methods can also be overloaded.

Summary

In this chapter you learned how to create objects in C# using the **new** keyword, how objects are stored in memory, how classes can be organized into namespaces, how to use access control to achieve encapsulation, and how C# manages unused objects. In addition, you learned about method overloading and static class members.

Chapter 5
Core Classes

Before discussing other object-oriented programming (OOP) features, let's examine several important classes that are commonly used in C#. These classes are included in the class library that come with the .NET Framework. Mastering them will help you understand the examples that accompany the next OOP lessons.

The most prominent class of all is definitely **System.Object**. However, it is hard to talk about this class without first covering inheritance, which we will do in Chapter 6, "Inheritance." Therefore, **System.Object** is only discussed briefly in this chapter. Right now we will concentrate on classes that you can use in your programs. We'll start with **System.String** and **System.Text.StringBuffer**. Then, we'll discuss arrays and the **System.Console** class. The complete documentation for these classes and other types in the .NET Framework class library is available online here.

```
http://msdn.microsoft.com/en-us/library/gg145045
```

System.Object

The **System.Object** class represents a C# object. In fact, all classes are direct or indirect descendants of this class. Since we have not learned inheritance (which is only given in Chapter 6, "Inheritance"), the word descendant probably makes no sense to you. Therefore, we will briefly discuss some of the methods in this class and revisit this class in Chapter 6.

Here are some of the methods in the **Object** class.

```
public boolean Equals(Object obj)
```

Compares this object with the passed-in object. A class must implement this method to provide a means to compare the contents of its instances.

```
public Type GetType()
```
Returns a **System.Type** object of this object. See the section "System.Type" for more information on the **Type** class later in this chapter.

```
public virtual int GetHashCode()
```
Returns a hash code value for this object.

```
public virtual string ToString()
```
Returns the string description of this object.

Do not worry about the keyword **virtual** used in some method signatures for now.

System.String

I have not seen a serious C# program that does not use the **System.String** class. It is one of the most often used classes and definitely one of the most important.

A **String** object represents a string, i.e. a piece of text. You can also think of a **String** as a sequence of Unicode characters. A **String** object can consists of any number of characters. A **String** that has zero character is called an empty **String**. **String** objects are constant. Once they are created, their values cannot be changed. Because of this, **String** instances are said to be immutable.

You could construct a **String** object using the **new** keyword and one of the **String** class's constructors, but this is not common. Most often, you simply assign a string literal to a **String** variable.

```
System.String s = ".NET is cool";
```

This produces a **String** object containing ".NET is cool" and assigns a reference to it to **s**.

An even easier way to create a **String** is by using the **string** type, an alias for the **String** class. The statement above can be rewritten more concisely like this.

```
string s = ".NET is cool";
```

A string can include characters that are escape sequences (that we learned in Chapter 2, "Language Fundamentals"), like this:

```
string fileName = "C:\\win.txt";
```

fileName will contain the value of C:\win.txt because \\ represents the backslash character. The following will raise an error because the compiler does not know what \w is.

```
string wrongFileName = "C:\win.txt";
```

You can, however, force the compiler to parse string literals differently by prefixing them with @. For example, the following is correct because \ is not considered the escape character but is regarded as a normal character.

```
String myFileName = @"C:\win.txt";
```

String Concatenation

You can concatenate two strings by using the + operator or the **String** class's **Concat** method.

Here is an example of using the + operator. After the following statements are executed, **greeting** will contain "Aloha".

```
string al = "Al";
string oha = "oha";
string greeting = al + oha;
```

Alternatively, you can use the **String** class's **Concat** method to concatenate two strings:

```
string al = "Al";
string oha = "oha";
string greeting = String.Concat(al, oha);
```

Note that since **Concat** is a static method, you can call it without first creating a **String** object.

Comparing Two Strings

String comparison is one of the most useful operations in C# programming. Consider the following code.

```
string a = ".NET is cool";
string b = a;
```

Here, **(a == b)** evaluates to **true** because **a** and **b** reference the same instance.

String Literals

Because you always work with **String** objects, it is important to understand the rules for working with string literals.

First of all, a string literal starts and ends with a double quote ("). Second, it is a compile error to change line before the closing ". For example, this will raise a compile error.

```
string s2 = "This is an important
        point to note";
```

You can compose long string literals by using the plus sign to concatenate two string literals.

```
string s1 = "Strings " + "are important";
string s2 = "This is an important " +
        "point to note";
```

You can concatenate a string with a primitive or another object. For instance, this line of code concatenates a **String** and an integer.

```
string s3 = "String number " + 3;
```

If an object is concatenated with a string, the **ToString** method of the former will be called and the result used in the concatenation.

Escaping Certain Characters

You sometimes need to use special characters in your strings such as carriage return (CR) and linefeed (LF). In other occasions, you may want to have a double quote character in your string. In the case of CR and LF, it is not possible to input these characters because pressing Enter changes lines. A way to include special characters is to escape them, i.e. use the character replacement for them.

Here are some escape sequences:

```
\u          /* a Unicode character
\b          /* \u0008: backspace BS */
\t          /* \u0009: horizontal tab HT */
\n          /* \u000a: new line */
\f          /* \u000c: form feed FF */
\r          /* \u000d: carriage return CR */
\"          /* \u0022: double quote " */
\'          /* \u0027: single quote ' */
\\          /* \u005c: backslash \ */
```

For example, the following code includes the Unicode character 0122 at the end of the string.

```
string s = "Please type this character \u0122";
```

To obtain a string whose value is John "The Great" Monroe, you escape the double quotes:

```
string s = "John \"The Great\" Monroe";
```

The String Class's Properties

The **String** class offers two properties, **Length** and **Chars**. The **Length** property provides the number of characters in the current **String** object. For example, the following line of code sets the **stringLength** variable to 5 because the number of characters in "Hello" is five.

```
int stringLength = "Hello".Length;
```

The **Chars** property returns the **Char** object at a specified index. The syntax of the **Chars** property is as follows.

```
public char this[int index] { get; }
```

Here, *index* indicates a zero-based position. Therefore, to get the first character in a string, you pass 0. For example, in the following code **greeting[0]** returns 'W'.

```
String greeting = "Welcome";
char firstChar = greeting[0];
```

Consequently, the **Chars** property will only accept 0 to the number of characters minus one. You'll get an **IndexOutOfRangeException** if you pass a number beyond that range.

As an example, the following code uses the **Length** and **Chars** properties to print individual characters in a string.

```
string greeting2 = "Hello";
for (int i = 0; i < greeting2.Length; i++)
{
    Console.WriteLine(greeting2[i]);
}
```

The String Class's Methods

The **String** class provides methods for manipulating the value of a **String**. However, since **String** objects are immutable, the result of the manipulation is always a new **String** object.

Here are some of the more useful methods.

```
public static string Concat(string s1, string s2)
```
> Concatenates two strings. For example, **String.Concat("Hello", "World")** returns "HelloWorld".

```
public bool Contains(string value)
```
> Indicates whether the current string contains the passed-in value. For example, **"Credit card".Contains("card")** returns true.

```
public bool EndsWith(string suffix)
```
> Tests if the current string ends with the specified suffix.

```
public int IndexOf(String substring)
```
Returns the index of the first occurrence of the specified substring. If no match is found, returns -1. For instance, the following expression returns 6.

```
"C# is cool".IndexOf("cool")
```

```
public int IndexOf(String substring, int fromIndex)
```
Returns the index of the first occurrence of the specified substring starting from the specified index. If no match is found, returns -1.

```
public int LastIndexOf(String substring)
```
Returns the index of the last occurrence of the specified substring. If no match is found, returns -1.

```
public int LastIndexOf(String substring, int fromIndex)
```
Returns the index of the last occurrence of the specified substring starting from the specified index. If no match is found, returns -1. For example, the following expression returns 7, which is the zero-based position of the last 'c'.

```
"credit card".LastIndexOf("c")
```

```
public string Substring(int beginIndex)
```
Returns a substring of the current string starting from the specified index. For instance, **"C# is cool".Substring(6)** returns "cool".

```
public string Substring(int beginIndex, int length)
```
Returns a substring of the current string starting from *beginIndex* . The returned string will have the specified length. For example, the following code returns "is":

```
"C# is cool".Substring(3, 2)
```

```
public string Replace(char oldChar, char newChar)
```
Replaces every occurrence of *oldChar* with *newChar* in the current string and returns a new string. **"dingdong".Replace('d', 'k')** returns "kingkong".

```
public string Replace(string oldValue, string newValue)
```
Replaces every occurrence of *oldValue* with *newValue* in the current string and returns a new string. the number of characters in this **String**. For example, **"Spring".Replace("Spr", "st")** returns "sting".

```
public static bool IsNullOrEmpty(string value)
```
Returns true is the specified string is null or empty. An empty string contains no characters.

```
public string[] Split(char[] separator)
```
Splits the current string around matches of the specified character array. For example, **"big city mayors".Split(" ")** returns an array of three strings. The first array element is "big", the second "city", and the third "mayors".

```
public bool StartsWith(String prefix)
```
Tests if the current string starts with the specified prefix.

```
public char[] ToCharArray()
```
Returns the current string as a char array.

```
public string ToLower()
```
Converts all the characters in the current string to lower case. For instance, **"Coffee shop hero".ToLower()** returns "coffee shop hero".

```
public String ToUpper()
```
Converts all the characters in the current string to upper case. For instance, **"temporary".ToUpper()** returns "TEMPORARY".

```
public string Trim()
```
Trims the trailing and leading white spaces and returns a new string. For example, **" Venus ".Trim()** returns "Venus".

System.Text.StringBuilder

String objects are immutable and are not a good choice if you need to append or insert characters into them. This is because string operations on **String** always create a new **String** object and are therefore expensive. For modern computers, the "cost" in additional processing time is likely negligible. However, it is good programming practice to avoid such operations. For append and insert, you'd be better off using the **System.Text.StringBuilder** class.

To use **StringBuilder**, you start by creating an instance, specifying a capacity, which is the number of characters it can contain. When you append a character or a string to your **StringBuilder**, the system does not create a new instance as long as there is still enough room for the addition. If you exceed the capacity, the system will automatically increase the capacity but at a cost. Therefore, you should make sure you create a **StringBuilder** with enough capacity, but not too big as each reserved character space, even if not used, takes memory space. Once you're finished manipulating the string, you can convert a **StringBuilder** to a string.

Let's now look at how you can create a **StringBuilder** and use its methods.

StringBuilder Class's Constructors

The **StringBuilder** class has five constructors. The simplest one is the no-argument constructor that creates a **StringBuilder** with a capacity of 16 characters.

```
public StringBuilder()
```

The second constructor allows you to specify a capacity:

```
public StringBuilder(int capacity)
```

There is also a constructor that allows you to set a maximum capacity. Trying to add more characters than the maximum capacity will result in an exception being thrown.

```
public StringBuilder(int capacity, int maximumCapacity)
```

You can prepopulate a StringBuilder with a string if you wish, using the fourth constructor.

```
public StringBuilder(string value)
```

And, you can specify an initial string and a capacity using the fifth:

```
public StringBuilder(string value, int capacity)
```

Finally, the last constructor of StringBuilder allows you to use a substring as an initial value.

```
public StringBuilder(string value, int startIndex, int length,
        int capacity)
```

For example, the following statement creates a **StringBuilder** with "World" as its initial value:

```
string s = "Hello World";
StringBuilder builder = new StringBuilder(s, 6, 5, 20);
```

A **StringBuilder** created without specifying a maximum capacity will have a very large capacity (2 gigabytes).

StringBuilder Class's Properties

The **StringBuilder** class offers four properties: **Capacity**, **Chars**, **Length**, and **MaximumCapacity**:

```
public int Capacity { get; set; }
```
> The capacity of the **StringBuilder**.

```
public char this[int index] {get; set; }
```
> Gets or sets the character at the specified index. For example, the following code creates a **StringBuilder** and changes the first and fifth characters.
>
> ```
> StringBuilder builder4 = new StringBuilder("Kingkong");
> builder4[0] = 'P';
> builder4[4] = 'p';
> ```

```
public int Length { get; set; }
```
> Gets or sets the length of this **StringBuilder**.

```
public int MaxCapacity { get; }
```
> Retrieves the maximum capacity of this **StringBuilder**.

StringBuilder Class's Methods

Without a doubt the most important method in **StringBuilder** is its **ToString** method, which returns the content of a StringBuilder as a string:

```
public override string ToString()
```

Without this method, the **StringBuilder** class will be almost useless because while countless methods take string arguments, few accept a **StringBuilder**.

StringBuilder also defines methods for appending, inserting, and removing a character in a **StringBuilder** instance. The **Append** method comes with multiple overloads to make it possible to append a string, a character, a number, or another data type. If you append an integer, the integer will be converted to a char before being appended.

Like **Append**, the **Insert** method is also available in multiple overloads to allow you to insert different data types to a **StringBuilder**. The difference between **Append** and **Insert** is that **Append** always adds a character at the end of the **StringBuilder** whereas **Insert** lets you adds a character at any position.

Here are some overloads of **Append** and **Insert**.

```
public StringBuilder Append(string value)

public StringBuilder Append(char value)

public StringBuilder Append(Object value)

public StringBuilder Append(int value)

public StringBuilder Insert(int index, string value)

public StringBuilder Insert(int index, char value)

public StringBuilder Insert(int index, Object value)

public StringBuilder Insert(int index, int value)
```

In addition to **Append** and **Insert**, **StringBuilder** also provides a **Remove** method to remove characters:

```
public StringBuilder Remove(int startIndex, int length)
```

What's interesting is that **Append**, **Insert**, and **Remove** all return the same **StringBuilder** so that the methods can be chained like this.

```
StringBuilder sb = new StringBuilder("Hi Hello");
sb.Append("World").Insert(8, ' ').Remove(0, 3);
Console.WriteLine(sb.ToString()); // print "Hello World"
```

Arrays

In C# you can use arrays to group primitives or objects of the same type. The entities belonging to an array is called the elements or members of the array. An array is an instance of a class derived from **System.Array**. Therefore, an array inherits all the fields, properties, and methods of the **System.Array** class. For example, you can call the **Length** field on your array to get the number of elements in it. The **Length** field is a field defined in **System.Array**.

All elements of an array have the same type, called the *element type* of the array. An array is not resizable and an array with zero component is called an empty array.

An array is an object. Therefore, you treat a variable that refers to an array like other reference variables. For one, you can compare it with **null**.

```
String[] names;
if (names == null)  // evaluates to true
```

Note
An array can also contain other arrays, creating an array of arrays.

You use this syntax to declare an array:

```
type[] arrayName;
```

For example, the following declares an array of **long**s named **numbers**:

```
long[] numbers;
```

Declaring an array does not create an array or allocate space for its components, the compiler simply creates an object reference. One way to create an array is by using the **new** keyword. You must specify the size of the array you are creating.

```
new type[size]
```

As an example, the following code creates an array of four **int**s:

```
new int[4]
```

Alternatively, you can declare and create an array in the same line.

```
int[] ints = new int[4];
```

To reference the components of an array, use an index after the variable name. Arrays are zero-based, which means the first element of an array is indexed 0. To retrieve an element of an array, you use its index in brackets. For example, the following snippet creates an array of four **String** objects and initializes its first member.

```
string[] names = new string[4];
names[0] = "Hello World"; //assign value to first element of names
```

You can also create and initialize an array without using the **new** keyword. For example, the following code creates an array of three **String** objects.

```
String[] names = { "John", "Mary", "Paul" };
```

The following code creates an array of four **int**s and assign the array to the variable **matrix**.

```
int[] matrix = { 1, 2, 3, 10 };
```

Be careful when passing an array to a method because the following is illegal even though the average method below take an array of **int**s.

```
int avg = average( { 1, 2, 3, 10 } ); // illegal
```

Instead, you have to instantiate the array separately.

```
int[] numbers = { 1, 2, 3, 10 };
int avg = average(numbers);
```

or this

```
int avg = average(new int[] { 1, 2, 3, 10 });
```

Referencing an out-of-range element will raise a runtime error. For example, the following code will raise an error because it tries to access the fifth element of an array that contains two elements:

```
int[] numbers = { 1, 3 };
int x = numbers[4];
```

Note
When an array is created, its elements are either **null** (if the element type is an object type) or the default value of the element type (if the array contains primitives). For example, an array of **int**s contains zeros by default.

Iterating over an Array

There are two ways of iterating over an array, by using **foreach** and **for**. The former is has a shorter format:

```
foreach (elementType element in arrayName)
{
    // access element here
}
```

For example, the following snippet prints the elements in **employees**.

```
string[] employees = { "John", "Paul", "George", "Ringo" };
foreach (string employee in employees)
{
    Console.WriteLine("Employee:" + employee); // print employee
}
```

The result is as follows.

```
Employee:John
Employee:Paul
Employee:George
Employee:Ringo
```

The second method is to use the **for** loop and access each element by its index:

```
string[] employees = { "John", "Paul", "George", "Ringo" };
for (int i = 0; i < employees.Length; i++)
{
    Console.WriteLine("Employee(" + (i + 1) + "): " + employees[i]);
}
```

Here is the result.

```
Employee(1):John
Employee(2):Paul
```

```
Employee(3):George
Employee(4):Ringo
```

You see, even though **foreach** is simpler, sometimes you resort to the for loop if the indexes are important to you.

Changing an Array Size

Once an array is created, its size cannot be changed. If you want to change the size, you must create a new array and populates it using the values of the old array. For instance, the following code increases the size of **numbers**, an array of three **int**s, to 4.

```
int[] numbers = { 1, 2, 3 };
int[] temp = new int[4];
for (int j = 0; j < numbers.Length; j++)
{
    temp[j] = numbers[j];
}
numbers2 = temp;
```

Alternatively, you can use the **Resize** static method of **System.Array**:

```
Array.Resize(ref arrayName, newSize)
```

As an example, the following code changes the size of **numbers** to 5.

```
int[] numbers = { 2, 3, 4 };
Array.Resize(ref numbers, 5);
Console.WriteLine("Length of numbers:" + numbers.Length);
```

Passing a String Array to Main

You may pass a string array to the **Main** method to feed values to your program. In this case, here is the signature of the **Main** method:

```
public static void Main(string[] args)
```

Listing 5.1 shows a class that iterates over the **Main** method's **String** array argument.

Listing 5.1: Accessing the Main method's arguments

```
public class MainMethodTest
{
    public static void main(String[] args) {
        foreach (string arg in args) {
            Console.WriteLine(arg);
        }
    }
}
```

System.Console

The **System.Console** class exposes useful static fields and static methods to work with the console. Here are some of the more important methods in **System.Console**.

```
public static void Beep()
```
Plays the sound of a beep.

```
public static void Clear()
```
Clears the console buffer and the console window.

```
public static ConsoleKeyInfo ReadKey()
```
Gets the information about the next key pressed by the user and display it in the console window.

```
public static string ReadLine()
```
Returns the next line of characters from the input stream.

```
public static void Write(string s)
```
Writes the string argument to the console. There are other Write overloads so you can pass any type to **Write**.

```
public static void WriteLine(string s)
```
Writes the string argument plus the line terminator to the console.

Summary

In this chapter you have examined several important classes such as **System.Object**, **System.String**, **System.Text.StringBuilder**,

System.Array, and **System.Console**. These are some of the most frequently used classes in C#. You will learn about more classes in the next chapters.

Chapter 6
Inheritance

Inheritance is a very important object-oriented programming (OOP) feature. It is what makes code extensible in any OOP language. Extending a class is also called inheriting or subclassing. In C#, by default all classes are extendible, but you can use the **sealed** keyword to prevent a class from being subclassed. This chapter explains inheritance in C#.

An Overview of Inheritance

You extend a class by creating a new class. The former and the latter will then have a parent-child relationship. The original class is the parent class or the base class or the superclass. The new class is the child class or the subclass or the derived class of the parent. The process of extending a class in OOP is called inheritance. In a subclass you can add new methods, new fields, and new properties as well as override existing methods to change their behaviors.

Figure 6.1 presents a UML class diagram that depicts a parent-child relationship between a class and a child class.

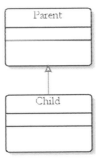

Figure 6.1: The UML class diagram for a parent class and a child class

Note that a line with an arrow is used to depict generalization, e.g. a parent-child relationship.

A child class in turn can be extended, unless you specifically make it inextensible by declaring it sealed. Sealed classes are discussed in the section "Sealed Classes" later in this chapter.

The benefits of inheritance are obvious. Inheritance gives you the opportunity to add some functionality that does not exist in the original class. It also gives you the chance to change the behaviors of the existing class to better suit your needs.

Extending A Class

You extend a class by using the colon in the class declaration, after the class name and before the parent class. Listing 6.1 presents a class named **Parent** and Listing 6.2 a class named **Child** that extends **Parent**.

Listing 6.1: The Parent class

```
public class Parent
{

}
```

Listing 6.2: The Child class

```
public class Child : Parent
{

}
```

Extending a class is as simple as that.

> **Note**
> All classes in C# automatically extend the **System.Object** class. **Object** is the ultimate superclass in .NET. **Parent** in Listing 6.1 by default is a subclass of **Object**.

> **Note**
> In C# a class can only extend one other class. This is unlike C++ where multiple inheritance is allowed. However, the notion of

multiple inheritance can be achieved by using interfaces, as discussed in Chapter 9, "Interfaces and Abstract Classes."

The is-a Relationship

There is a special relationship that is formed when you create a new class by inheritance. The subclass and the superclass has an "is-a" relationship.

For example, **Animal** is a class that represents animals. There are many types of animals, including birds, fish, and dogs, so you can create subclasses of **Animal** that represent specific types of animals. Figure 6.2 features the **Animal** class with three subclasses, **Bird**, **Fish**, and **Dog**.

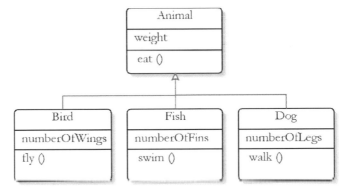

Figure 6.2: An example of inheritance

The is-a relationship between the subclasses and the superclass **Animal** is very apparent. A bird "is an" animal, a dog is an animal, and a fish is an animal. A subclass is a special type of its superclass. For example, a bird is a special type of animal. The is-a relationship does not go the other way, however. An animal is not necessarily a bird or a dog.

Listing 6.3 presents the **Animal** class and its subclasses.

Listing 6.3: Animal and its subclasses

```
class Animal
{
    public float Weight;
    public void Eat()
```

```
        {
        }
    }
    class Bird : Animal {
        public int NumberOfWings = 2;
        public void Fly()
        {
        }
    }
    class Fish : Animal {
        public int NumberOfFins = 2;
        public void Swim()
        {
        }
    }
    class Dog : Animal {
        public int NumberOfLegs = 4;
        public void Walk()
        {
        }
    }
```

In this example, the **Animal** class defines a **Weight** field that applies to all animals. It also declares an **Eat** method because animals eat.

The **Bird** class is a special type of **Animal**, it inherits the **Eat** method and the **Weight** field. **Bird** also adds a **NumberOfWings** field and a **Fly** method. This shows that the more specific **Bird** class extends the functionality and behavior of the more generic **Animal** class.

A subclass inherits all public methods and fields of its superclass. For example, you can create a **Dog** object and call its **Eat** method:

```
Dog dog = new Dog();
dog.Eat();
```

The **Eat** method is declared in the **Animal** class; the **Dog** class simply inherits it.

A consequence of the is-a relationship is that it is legal to assign an instance of a subclass to a reference variable of the parent type. For example, the following code is valid because **Bird** is a subclass of **Animal**, and a **Bird** is always an **Animal**.

```
Animal animal = new Bird();
```

However, the following is illegal because there is no guarantee that an **Animal** would be a **Dog.**:

```
Dog dog = new Animal();
```

Accessibility

From within a subclass you can access its superclass's public and protected members, such as methods and fields, but not the superclass's private members. If the subclass and the superclass are in the same assembly, you can also access the superclass's internal members.

Consider the **P** and **C** classes in Listing 6.4.

Listing 6.4: Showing accessibility

```
public class P
{
    public void PublicMethod()
    {
    }

    protected void ProtectedMethod()
    {
    }

    internal void InternalMethod()
    {
    }
}

class C : P
{
    public void TestMethods()
    {
        PublicMethod();
        ProtectedMethod();
        InternalMethod();
    }
}
```

P has three methods, one public, one protected, and one with internal access level. **C** is a subclass of **P**. As you can see in the **C** class's **TestMethods** method, **C** can access its parent's public and protected method. In addition, because **C** and **P** are in the same assembly, **C** can also access **P**'s internal method.

Method Overriding

When you extend a class, you can change the behavior of a method in the parent class. This is called method overriding, and this happens when you write in a subclass a method that has the same signature as a method in the parent class. If only the name is the same but the list of arguments is not, then it is method overloading. Method overloading was explained in Chapter 4, "Objects and Classes."

You override a method to change its behavior. To override a method, you write the new method in the subclass. You can override the superclass's public and protected methods. If the subclass and superclass are in the same assembly, you can also override a method with the internal access level.

An example of method overriding is demonstrated by the **Shape** and **Oval** classes in Listing 6.5.

Listing 6.5: The Shape and Oval classes

```
using System;
class Shape
{
    public void WhatAmI()
    {
        Console.WriteLine("I am a shape");
    }

}

class Oval : Shape
{
    new public void WhatAmI()
    {
        Console.WriteLine("I am an oval");
    }
}
```

The **Oval** class extends **Shape** and overrides the **WhatAmI** method. The **new** keyword is used in the subclass to indicate that the programmer is aware that the **WhatAmI** method in the parent class is overridden. Without the **new** keyword, the program will still compile, but with a warning.

You can test the method overriding in Listing 6.5 with the following code.

```
Oval oval = new Oval();
oval.WhatAmI(); // prints "I am an oval"
```

As you can see, **oval.WhatAmI** invokes the method in the **Oval** class.

Now guess, what would be the output of this snippet?

```
Shape shape = new Oval();
shape.WhatAmI();
```

Assigning an object variable with an instance of its subclass is legal in C# because, after all, an oval is a shape. However, the output might surprise you. It is

```
I am a shape
```

In C# calling a method using a reference variable invokes the method defined in the type, regardless the type of object the reference variable refers to.

Calling the Base Class's Constructors

A subclass is just like an ordinary class, you use the **new** keyword to create an instance of it. If you do not explicitly write a constructor in your subclass, the compiler will implicitly add a no-argument (no-arg) constructor.

When you instantiate a child class by invoking one of its constructors, the first thing the constructor does is call the default constructor (the one that takes no argument) of the direct parent class. In the parent class, the constructor also calls the constructor of its direct parent class. This process repeats itself until the constructor of the **System.Object** class is reached. In other words, when you create a child object, all its parent classes are also instantiated.

This process is illustrated in the **Employee** and **Manager** classes in Listing 6.6.

Listing 6.6: Calling a base class's default constructor

```csharp
using System;
class Employee
{
    public Employee()
    {
        Console.WriteLine("Employee()");
    }
    public Employee(string name)
    {
        Console.WriteLine("Employee() " + name);
    }
}

class Manager : Employee
{
    public Manager(string name)
    {
        Console.WriteLine("Manager() " + name);
    }
}
```

If you instantiate the **Manager** class as in the following code

```csharp
Manager manager = new Manager("Jeff");
```

You'll see this in your console.

```
Employee
Manager() Jeff
```

This proves that the first thing that the **Employee** class's constructor does is invoke the **Employee** class's default constructor even when there is another constructor with the same set of arguments.

To invoke a non-default constructor in the base class when creating an instance of a subclass, you can use the **base** keyword. For example, change the constructor in **Manager** to the following to invoke the second constructor in **Employee**:

```
public Manager(string name) : base(name)
{
    Console.WriteLine("Manager() " + name);
}
```

Note that it makes sense for a child class to call its parent's constructor from its own constructor because an instance of a subclass must always be accompanied by an instance of each of its parents. This way, calls to a method that is not overridden in a child class will be passed to its parent until the first in the hierarchy is found.

Calling the Base Class's Hidden Members

The **base** keyword has another purpose in life. It can be used to call a hidden member or an overridden method in a base class. Since **base** represents an instance of the direct parent, base.*memberName* returns the specified member in the parent class. You can access any member in the base class that is visible from the subclass. For example, Listing 6.8 shows two classes that have a parent-child relationship: **Tool** and **Pencil**.

Listing 6.8: Using super to access a hidden member

```
using System;
public class Tool
{
    public string Identify()
    {
        return "Generic tool";
    }
}

public class Pencil : Tool {
    new public string Identify()
    {
        return "Pencil";
    }

    public void Write()
    {
        Console.WriteLine(base.Identify());
```

```
        Console.WriteLine(Identify());
    }

}
```

The **Pencil** class overrides the **Identify** method in **Tool**. If you instantiate
the **Pencil** class and call its **Write** method, you will see the following on the
console.

```
Generic tool
Pencil
```

Type Casting

You can cast an object to another type. The rule is, you can only cast an
instance of a subclass to its parent class. Casting an object to a parent class
is called upcasting. Here is an example, assuming that **Child** is a subclass of
Parent.

```
Child child = new Child();
Parent parent = child;
```

To upcast a **Child** object, all you need to do is assign the object to a
reference variable of type **Parent**. Note that the **parent** reference variable
cannot access the members that are only available in **Child**.

Because **parent** in the snippet above references an object of type **Child**,
you can cast it back to **Child**. This time, it is called downcasting because
you are casting an object to a class down the inheritance hierarchy.
Downcasting requires that you write the child type in brackets. For
example:

```
Child child = new Child();
Parent parent = child;// parent pointing to an instance of Child
Child child2 = (Child) parent; // downcasting
```

Downcasting to a subclass is only allowed if the parent class reference is
already pointing to an instance of the subclass. The following will generate
a compile error.

```
Object parent = new Object();
Child child = (Child) parent; // illegal downcasting, compile error
```

Sealed Classes

You can prevent others from extending your class by making it sealed using the keyword **sealed** in the class declaration. **sealed** may appear after or before the access modifier. For example:

```
public final class Pencil
final public class Pen
```

The first form is more common.

Even though making a class sealed makes your code slightly faster, the difference is too insignificant to notice. Design consideration, and not speed, should be the reason you make a class final. For example, the **System.String** class is sealed because the designer of the class did not want you to change the behavior of the **String** class.

The is Keyword

The **is** keyword can be used to test if an object is of a specified type. It is normally used in an **if** statement and its syntax is.

```
if (objectReference is type)
```

where *objectReference* references an object being investigated. For example, the following **if** statement returns **true**.

```
String s = "Hello";
if (s is System.String)
```

However, applying **is** on a **null** reference variable returns **false**. For example, the following **if** statement returns **false**.

```
String s = null;
if (s is System.String)
```

Also, since a subclass "is a" type of its base class, the following **if** statement, where **Child** is a subclass of **Parent**, returns **true**.

```
Child child = new Child();
```

```
if (child is Parent)     // evaluates to true
```

Summary

Inheritance is one of the fundamental principles in object-oriented programming. Inheritance makes code extensible. In C# all classes by default extend the **System.Object** class. To extend a class, use the colon. Method overriding is another OOP feature directly related to inheritance. It enables you to change the behavior of a member in the parent class. You can prevent your class from being subclassed by making it sealed.

Chapter 7
Structures

In Introduction you learned that .NET types consists of classes, structures, enumerations, interfaces, and delegates. Classes were discussed in Chapter 4, "Objects and Classes" and you should be familiar with them by now.

The second type, structures or simply structs, are like classes, in which they can have members like fields and methods. Unlike classes, however, structures are value types and cannot inherit or be inherited. The .NET Framework class library offers many of them. For example, the **System** namespace defines important structures like **Byte**, **Char**, **Int32**, and **DateTime** that represent important data types.

This chapter explains what a structure is and shows a couple of examples.

An Overview of Structures

Sometimes called light-weight classes, structures, like classes, can have members such as fields and methods and you can use **new** to create an instance of a structure. However, structures are value types whereas classes are reference types. Value types are allocated on the stack or inline and deallocated when they go out of scope. On the other hand, reference types are allocated on the heap and unused instances of reference types are garbage-collected. Value types are generally cheaper to create but perform more poorly than reference types if they are involved in a lot of boxing and unboxing. All structures are implicitly derived from **System.ValueType**.

Unlike classes, structures cannot have children. In other words, structures do not support inheritance.

.NET Structures

The .NET Framework comes with a lot of structures. All primitive types in C#, such as **int** and **char**, are aliases to structures defined in the **System** namespace. For example, every time you declare an **int** in your C# code, an instance of **System.Int32** is created. Every time you use a **char**, there is a **System.Char** instance backing it up. As such, you can call the members of the corresponding structure on your primitive as illustrated in the following snippet.

```
int a = 123;
System.Console.WriteLine(a.GetType()); // prints System.Int32
```

Another difference between structures and classes is the fact that it is not possible for two variables to point to the same structure instance. Assigning a structure to a new variable creates a new instance of the structure. In Listing 7.1 the **System.Numerics.Complex** structure, which represents complex numbers, is used to prove the point.

Note that **System.Numerics** namespace can be found in the **System.Numerics.dll** assembly, and to use its members you need to first add a reference to the assembly in your project. See the sidebar on how to add an assembly to a project.

Adding A Reference to A Project

When you create a project in Visual Studio or a similar IDE, several assemblies are included by default. You don't need to do anything to use types in the assemblies. If you want to use a type that is not in the default assemblies, you need to reference the assembly in your project by following these steps:

1. In Solution Explorer, select the project you want to add a reference to.

2. On the Project menu, choose **Add Reference**.

3. In the **Add Reference** dialog that appears, select the tab indicating the type of component you want to reference.

4. In the top pane, select the component to reference and then click the **Select** button.

Listing 7.1: Copying a structure

```
using System;
using System.Numerics;

class Numerics
{
    public void Test()
    {
        Complex c1 = new Complex(2d, 3);
        // creates a new copy of c1
        Complex c2 - c1;
        c2 *= c2; // does not affect c1
        Console.WriteLine(c1); // prints (2, 3)
        Console.WriteLine(c2); // prints (-5, 12)
    }
}
```

If you run **Test()**, you'll see the following on the console:

```
(2, 3)
(-5, 12)
```

This proves that **c1** and **c2** represent two different objects because when you assign **c1** to **c2**, a new copy of **Complex** is created. Therefore, manipulating **c2** does not affect **c1** and vice versa.

Writing A Structure

The following section shows how to write a custom structure. You use the keyword **struct** followed by the struct name to create a structure. Listing 7.2 shows the code of a custom struct named **Point**. The struct has two fields (X and Y) and two methods, **Move** and **Print**.

Listing 7.2: A custom structure

```
struct Point
```

```
{
    public int X;
    public int Y;

    public void Move(int x, int y)
    {
        X += x;
        Y += y;
    }

    public void Print()
    {
        System.Console.WriteLine("(" + X + ", " + Y + ")");
    }
}
```

The following code can be used to test the **Point** structure.

```
Point point1 = new Point();
point1.Print();// prints (0, 0)
point1.X = 10;
point1.Y = 20;
point1.Move(4, 5);
point1.Print(); // prints (14, 25)
```

Nullable Types

Another big difference between reference types and value types is that reference types can be null and value types cannot. Therefore, declaring a class variable to **null** is valid in C#:

```
string name = null;
```

However, assigning **null** to a structure variable raises a compile error. For example, **System.DateTime** is a structure, and the following code won't compile because it's illegal to assign **null** to a structure.

```
System.DateTime today = null;
```

The inability to assign null to a value type often causes a headache especially when working with a relational database where a table column can be null, which means it does not contain data. Retrieving a date from the database and assigning it to a **System.DateTime** can be problematic if the database date can be null. To get around this, the .NET Framework provides the **System.Nullable** structure to make any structure nullable. The beauty of this solution is that you don't have to work with **System.Nullable** directly. To make a structure nullable, simply append a question mark to the type name:

```
int? x = null; // x is nullable
```

Summary

In this chapter you learned about structures and how they differ from classes. You also learned the differences between value types and reference types and wrote a custom structure.

Chapter 8
Error Handling

Error handling is an important feature in any programming language. A good error handling mechanism makes it easier for programmers to write robust applications and to prevent bugs from creeping in. In some languages, programmers are forced to use multiple **if** statements to detect all possible conditions that might lead to an error. This could make code excessively complex. In a larger program, this practice could easily lead to spaghetti like code.

C# has a very nice approach to error handling by using the **try** statement. With this strategy, part of the code that could potentially lead to an error is isolated in a block. Should an error occur, this error is caught and resolved locally. This chapter explain C# error handling.

Catching Exceptions

You can isolate code that may cause a runtime error using the **try** statement, which is normally accompanied by the **catch** and **finally** statements. Such isolation typically occurs in a method body. If an error is encountered, the common language runtime (CLR) stops the processing of the **try** block and jumps to the **catch** block. Here you can gracefully handle the error or notify the user by 'throwing' a **System.Exception** object. Another scenario is to re-throw the exception or a new **Exception** object back to the code that called the method. It is then up to the client how he or she would handle the error. If a thrown exception is not caught, the application will stop abruptly.

This is the syntax of the **try** statement.

```
try
{
```

```
    [code that may throw an exception]
}
[catch (ExceptionType-1 [e])
{
    [code that is executed when ExceptionType-1 is thrown]
}]
[catch (ExceptionType-2 [e])
{
    [code that is executed when ExceptionType-2 is thrown]
}]
  ...
[catch (ExceptionType-n [e])
{
    [code that is executed when ExceptionType-n is thrown]
}]
[finally
{
    [code that runs regardless of whether an exception was thrown]]
}]
```

The steps for error handling can be summarized as follows:

1. Isolate code that could lead to an error in a **try** block.
2. For each individual **catch** block, write code that is to be executed if an exception of that particular type occurs in the **try** block.
3. In the **finally** block, write code that will be run whether or not an error has occurred.

Note that the **catch** and **finally** blocks are optional, but one of them must exist. Therefore, you can have **try** with one or more **catch** blocks or **try** with **finally** or **try** with **catch** and **finally**.

The previous syntax shows that you can have more than one **catch** block. This is because some code can throw different types of exceptions. When an exception is thrown from a **try** block, control is passed to the first **catch** block. If the type of exception thrown matches or is a subclass of the exception in the first **catch** block, the code in the **catch** block is executed and then control goes to the **finally** block, if one exists.

If the type of the exception thrown does not match the exception type in the first **catch** block, the CLR goes to the next **catch** block and does the same thing until it finds a match. If no match is found, the exception object will be thrown to the method caller. If the caller does not put the offending code that calls the method in a **try** block, the program will crash.

To illustrate the use of this error handling, consider the **NumberDoubler** class in Listing 8.1. When the class is run, it will prompt you for input. You can type in anything, including non-digits. If your input is successfully converted to a number, it will double it and print the result. If your input is invalid, the program will print an "Invalid input" message.

Listing 8.1: The NumberDoubler class

```
using System;

class NumberDoubler
{
    public void Test()
    {
        Console.WriteLine("Please type a number"
            + " between 0 and 255 that you want to double");
        string input = Console.ReadLine();
        try
        {
            Byte number = Byte.Parse(input);
            Console.WriteLine("Result: {0}", 2 * number);
        }
        catch (FormatException e) {
            Console.WriteLine("Invalid input ");
            Console.WriteLine(e.StackTrace);
        }
        catch (OverflowException)
        {
            Console.WriteLine("The number you entered exceeded"
                    "capacity");
        }
    }
}
```

The **NumberDoubler** class uses the **System.Console** class to take user input.

```
string input = Console.ReadLine();
```

It then uses the static **Parse** method of the **System.Byte** structure to convert the string input to a **byte**. If you look at the documentation, this method can throw one of the following exceptions:

- **ArgumentNullException**, if the string input is null.
- **FormatException**, if the string input is not a number.
- **OverflowException**, if the string input is less than 0 or greater than 255.

The **Test** method in the **NumberDoubler** class does not try to catch the **ArgumentNullException** because the output from **Console.ReadLine()** is never null. Also note that the second **catch** block does not define a variable for **OverflowException** as the code in the block does not use it.

To test the **NumberDouble** class, write and run this code.

```
new NumberDoubler().Test();
```

You will see this on the console:

```
Please type a number between 0 and 255 that you want to double
```

If you type a number between 0 and 255, you'll see your number doubled. However, if you type a non-number, such as "abcd," the **Parse** method will throw a **FormatException** and you'll see an error message followed by the stack trace that tells you the cause of the error.

```
Invalid input.
   at System.Number.StringToNumber(String str, NumberStyles options,
       NumberBuffer& number, NumberFormatInfo info, Boolean
       parseDecimal)
   at System.Number.ParseInt32(String s, NumberStyles style,
       NumberFormatInfo info)
   at System.Byte.Parse(String s, NumberStyles style,
       NumberFormatInfo info)
   at System.Byte.Parse(String s)
   at NumberDoubler.Test() in C:\App08\NumberDoubler.cs:line 12
```

try without catch and the using Statement

A **try** statement can be used with **finally** without a catch block. You normally use this syntax to ensure that some code always gets executed whether or not the code in the **try** block can finish successfully. For example, after opening a database connection, you want to make sure its **Close** method is called after you're done with the connection. To illustrate this scenario, consider the following pseudocode that opens a database connection.

```
Connection connection = null;
try
{

    // open connection
    // do something with the connection and perform other tasks

}
finally {
    if (connection != null)
    {
        // close connection
        connection.Close();
    }
}
```

If something unexpected occurs in the **try** block and it throws an exception, the **Close** method will always be called to release the resource.

In C# the **using** statement (not to be confused with the **using** directive that is used to import a namespace) can be used as a convenient syntax to ensure that managed types that access unmanaged resources release the resources after use by calling the **Dispose** method of the managed types. Examples of managed types that access unmanaged resources are **File** and **Font**. When creating a file, for example, the **System.IO.File** class also create a stream object that lets you read from or write to the file. When you no longer need the file, the corresponding stream must be properly disposed. Employing the **using** statement allows you to write very short code like this:

```
using (FileStream fs = File.Create(fileName))
{
    // do something with the FileStream here
}
```

The alternative is to use a **try** and a **finally** blocks like this:

```
FileStream fileStream = null;
try
{
    fileStream = File.Create("C:/temp.txt");
    // do something with fileStream here
}
finally
{
    // dispose of fileStream here.
}
```

You'll see more examples on using the **using** statement in Chapter 14, "Input/Output."

The System.Exception Class

Erroneous code can throw any type of exception. For example, trying to parse an invalid argument may throw a **System.FormatException**, and calling a method on a null reference variable throws a **System.ArgumentNullException**. All .NET exception classes derive from the **System.Exception** class. It is therefore worthwhile to spend some time examining this class.

Among others, the **Exception** class has **Message** and **StackTrace** properties. **Message** contains the description of the exception and **StackTrace** the immediate frames on the call stack.

Most of the time a **try** block is accompanied by a **catch** block that catches the **System.Exception** in addition to other **catch** blocks. The **catch** block that catches **Exception** must appear last. If other **catch** blocks fail to catch the exception, the last **catch** will do that. Here is an example.

```
try
{
    // code
}
catch (FormatException e)
{
    // handle  FormatException
}
catch (Exception e)
{
```

```
    // handle other exceptions
}
```

You may want to use multiple **catch** blocks in the code above because the statements in the **try** block may throw a **FormatException** or other type of exception. If the latter is thrown, it will be caught by the last **catch** block.

Be warned, though: The order of the **catch** blocks is important. You cannot, for example, put a **catch** block for handling **System.Exception** before any other **catch** block. This is because the CLR tries to match the thrown exception with the argument of the **catch** blocks in the order of appearance. **System.Exception** catches everything; therefore, the **catch** blocks after it would never be executed.

If you have several **catch** blocks and the exception type of one of the **catch** blocks is derived from the type of another **catch** block, make sure the more specific exception type appears first.

Throwing an Exception from a Method

When catching an exception in a method, you have two options to handle the error that occurs inside the method. You can either handle the error in the method, thus quietly catching the exception without notifying the caller (this has been demonstrated in the previous examples), or you can throw the exception back to the caller and let the caller handle it. If you choose the second option, the calling code must catch the exception that is thrown back by the method.

Listing 8.2 presents a **Capitalize** method that changes the first letter of a **String** to upper case.

Listing 8.2: The Capitalize method

```
public string Capitalize(string s)
{
    if (s == null)
    {
        throw new ArgumentNullException(
            "Your passed a null argument");
    }
```

```
Character firstChar = s.charAt(0);
String theRest = s.substring(1);
return firstChar.toString().toUpperCase() + theRest;
}
```

If you pass null to **Capitalize**, it will throw a new
ArgumentNullException. Pay attention to the code that instantiates the
ArgumentNullException class and throws the instance:

```
throw new ArgumentNullException(
        "You passed a null argument");
```

The **throw** keyword is used to throw an exception. Don't confuse it with the
throws statement, which is used at the end of a method signature to indicate
that an exception of a given type may be thrown from the method.

The following example shows code that calls **Capitalize**.

```
String input = null;
try
{
    String capitalized = util.Capitalize(input);
    System.Console.WriteLine(capitalized);
}
catch (ArgumentNullException e)
{
    System.Console.Write(e.Message);
}
```

Note
A constructor can also throw an exception.

Final Note on Exception Handling

The **try** statement imposes some performance penalty. Therefore, do not use
it over-generously. If it is not hard to test for a condition, then you should
do the testing rather than depending on the **try** statement. For example,
calling a method on a null object throws an **ArgumentNullException**.
Therefore, you could always surround a method call with a **try** block:

```
try
{
    ref.MethodA();
```

. . .

However, it is not hard at all to check if **ref** is null prior to calling **MethodA**. Therefore, the following code is better because it eliminates the **try** block.

```
if (ref != null)
{
    ref.MethodA();
}
```

Summary

This chapter discussed the use of structured error handling and presented examples for each casc. You have also been introduced to the **System.Exception** class and its properties and methods.

Chapter 9
Numbers and Dates

In C# numbers are represented by types such as **byte**, **short**, **int**, **float**, **double**, and **long**. These C# types are aliases for .NET structures **System.Byte**, **System.Int16**, **System.Int32**, **System.Single**, **System.Double**, and **System.Int64**, respectively. In addition, dates are represented by the **System.DateTime** structure. When working with numbers and dates, three issues that you need to address are parsing, formatting, and manipulation.

Parsing deals with the conversion of a string into a number or a date. Parsing is commonplace because computer programs often require user input and user input is received as a string. If a program expects a number or a date but receives a string, then the string has to be first converted into a number or a date. Conversion is not always straightforward. Before conversion can take place, you first need to read the string and make sure it contains only characters that make up a number or a date. For example, "123abc" is not a number even though it starts with a number. "123.45" is a float, but not an integer. "12/25/2013" looks like a date, but it is only valid if the program is expecting a date in mm/dd/yyyy format. Converting a string to a number is called number parsing. Converting a string to a date is referred to as date parsing.

When you have a number or a date, you may want to display it in a specific format. For instance, 1000000 will be more readable if displayed as 1,000,000 and 12/25/2013 as Dec 25, 2013. These are number formatting and date formatting, respectively.

Number and date parsing and formatting are the topics of this chapter. These tasks can be easily achieved in .NET as the structures mentioned above provide relevant methods for this purpose. In addition, the **System.Math** class, which provides methods to perform mathematical operations, is also discussed. On top of that, there is a section on the **System.Calendar** class, a utility for manipulating dates.

Number Parsing

A C# program may require that the user input a number that will be processed or become an argument of a method. For example, a currency converter program would need the user to type in a value to be converted. You can use **ReadLine** method of the **System.Console** class to receive user input. However, the input will be a string, even though it contains digits only. Before you can work with the number, such as doubling it, you need to parse the string. The outcome of a successful number parsing is a number.

Therefore, the purpose of number parsing is to convert a string into a numeric value type. If parsing fails, for example because the string is not a number or a number outside the specified range, your program can throw an exception.

You can use the **Parse** method of any structure that represents a numeric type to parse a string. The return type of **Parse** is the same as the structure that contains the **Parse** method. For instance, the **Parse** method in **System.Int32** returns an **Int32**. If parsing fails, a **System.FormatException** is thrown.

As an example, the **NumberParsingTest** class in Listing 9.1 takes user input using **Console.ReadLine()** and parses it. If the user enters an invalid number, an error message will be displayed.

Listing 9.1: Parsing numbers (NumberParsingTest.cs)

```
using System;
namespace app09
{
    class NumberParsingTest
    {
        public static void Main()
        {
            Console.Write("Please type in a number:");
            String input = Console.ReadLine();
            try
```

```
        {
            int i = Int32.Parse(input);
            Console.WriteLine("The number entered: " + i);
        }
        catch (FormatException)
        {
            Console.WriteLine("Invalid user input");
        }
        Console.ReadKey();
    }
  }
}
```

Number Formatting

Number formatting helps make numbers more readable. For example, 1000000 is more readable if printed as 1,000,000 or 1.000.000. Which format you choose obviously depends on where you live. In the United States and English-speaking provinces of Canada, the comma is used to separate the thousands, whereas in France or Indonesia the dot is used. Therefore, number and date formatting depends on the culture (or locale) of the user. Fortunately, it's easy to handle culture information in .NET.

In .NET culture information, or culture info for short, is represented by the **System.Globalization.CultureInfo** class. A **CultureInfo** can be neutral (when it only specifies the language element of a culture) or specific (when both language and country are defined). It can also be an invariant culture if it is culture-insensitive.

The format for a culture name is the combination of an ISO 639 two-letter language code, a hyphen, and an ISO 3166 two-letter country code. Table 9.1 lists several language codes in ISO 639 and table 9.2 some of the country codes in ISO 3166 (http://userpage.chemie.fu-berlin.de/diverse/doc/ISO_3166.html).

Code	Language
de	German
el	Greek
en	English
es	Spanish
fr	French
hi	Hindi
it	Italian
ja	Japanese
nl	Dutch
pt	Portuguese
ru	Russian
zh	Chinese

Table 9.1: Examples of ISO 639 Language Codes

Country	Code
Australia	AU
Brazil	BR
Canada	CA
China	CN
Egypt	EG
France	FR
Germany	DE
India	IN
Mexico	MX
Switzerland	CH
Taiwan	TW
United Kingdom	GB
United States	US

Table 9.2: Examples of ISO 3166 Country Codes

For example, en-US is for English (United States), en-GB for English (United Kingdom), fr-FR for French (France), fr-CA for French (Canada), and jp-JA for Japanese (Japan). The only exceptions to this rule are zh-Hans (Chinese (Simplified)) and zh-Hant (Chinese (Traditional)), which both are neutral cultures.

The complete list of the supported culture info can be found here:

```
http://msdn.microsoft.com/en-us/goglobal/bb896001.aspx
```

For example, to construct a **CultureInfo** object representing the English language used in Canada, write this.

```
CultureInfo cInfo = new CultureInfo("en-CA");
```

Alternatively, you can use the static method **CreateSpecificCulture** in **CultureInfo**:

```
CultureInfo cInfo = CultureInfo.CreateSpecificCulture("en-CA");
```

Now that you have sufficient background information on culture info, let's delve into how you can format numbers in C#. The answer turns out to be simple, you use the **ToString** methods on the numeric types.

Here are the overloads of **ToString**.

```
public string ToString()
public string ToString(IFormatProvider provider)
public string ToString(string format)
public string ToString(string format, IformatProvider provider)
```

If you use the no-arg **ToString** method, the default system format will be used. If you live in the US, chances are it will be en-US. For example, the following **ToString** method formats the number 12345 as 12345, which is the same as the original form.

```
int value = 12345;
Console.WriteLine(value.ToString()); // prints 12345
```

The following code prints 2e3f (2×10^3) as 2000.

```
float floatValue = 2e3f; // 2 x 10^3
Console.WriteLine(floatValue.ToString()); //prints 2000
```

Depending on your need, the no-argument **ToString** method may or may not be good enough. If it is not, you can pass a format string to **ToString** using this method overload.

```
public string ToString(string format)
```

Here, you pass one of the standard numeric format strings given in Table 9.3

Format Specifier	Name
"C" or "c"	Currency
"D" or "d"	Decimal
"E" or "e"	Exponential
"F" or "f"	Fixed-point
"G" or "g"	General
"N" or "n"	Number
"P" or "p"	Percent
"R" or "r"	Round-trip
"X" or "x"	Hexadecimal

Table 9.3: Standard numeric format strings

More information on numeric format strings can be found here:

http://msdn.microsoft.com/en-us/library/dwhawy9k

For example, the following code prints 12345.

```
int intValue = 12345;
Console.WriteLine(intValue.ToString("g"));
```

Furthermore, if you live in the US or in a country that uses the same currency format as the US (and your computer is set to the default setting), you'll get $12,345.00 from this code snippet.

```
int intValue = 12345;
Console.WriteLine(intValue.ToString("c"));
```

In other words, in the absence of cultural information, the **ToString** method will assume the default. But, hey, what if you want to print something that is not your computer's default? Like, you're probably working for a client in another country? Then, you can use the other **ToString** overload that takes both format and culture information.

```
public string ToString(string format, IformatProvider provider)
```

Recall that **CultureInfo** implements **IFormatProvider**, so you can pass an instance of **CultureInfo** as the second argument. For instance, the following code prints 12345 as in currency format in French Canadian (i.e., the Province of Quebec):

```
CultureInfo frenchCanadian = new CultureInfo("fr-CA");
Console.WriteLine(intValue.ToString("c", frenchCanadian));
```

```
// prints 12 345,00 $
```

Regardless of your computer settings running the code above will give you **12 345,00 $**.

Listing 9.2 shows the **NumberFormatTest** class that demonstrates how to use various overloads of the **ToString** method to format a number.

Listing 9.2: The NumberFormatTest class

```
using System;
using System.Globalization;

namespace app09
{
    class NumberFormatTest
    {
        public static void Main()
        {
            float floatValue = 2e3f; // 2 x 10^3
            Console.WriteLine(floatValue.ToString()); //prints 2000
            int intValue = 12345;
            Console.WriteLine(intValue.ToString());

            // use format string
            Console.WriteLine(intValue.ToString("g"));
            //prints 12345
            Console.WriteLine(intValue.ToString("c"));
            //prints $12,345.00 if en-US


            CultureInfo frenchCanadian = new CultureInfo("fr-CA");
            Console.WriteLine(intValue.ToString("c",
                frenchCanadian)); // prints 12 345,00 $
            Console.ReadKey();
        }
    }
}
```

The System.Math Class

The **Math** class is a utility class that provides static methods for mathematical operations. There are also two static final double fields: **E** and **PI**. **E** represents the base of natural logarithms (e). Its value is close to 2.718. **PI** is the ratio of the circumference of a circle to its diameter (pi). Its value is 22/7 or approximately 3.1428.

Some of the methods in the **Math** class are given below.

```
public static double Abs(double a)
```
Returns the absolute value of the specified double..

```
public static double Acos(double a)
```
Returns the arc cosine of an angle, in the range of 0.0 through pi.

```
public static double Asin(double a)
```
Returns the arc sine of an angle, in the range of $-pi/2$ through pi/2.

```
public static double Atan(double a)
```
Returns the arc tangent of an angle, in the range of $-pi/2$ through pi/2.

```
public static double Cos(double a)
```
Returns the cosine of an angle.

```
public static double Exp(double a)
```
Returns Euler's number e raised to the power of the specified double.

```
public static double Log(double a)
```
Returns the natural logarithm (base e) of the specified double.

```
public static double Log10(double a)
```
Returns the base 10 logarithm of the specified double.

```
public static double Max(double a, double b)
```
Returns the greater of the two specified double values.

```
public static double Min(double a, double b)
```
Returns the smaller of the two specified double values.

Working with Dates and Times

There are at least two classes in the .NET Framework class library that can be used to work with dates and times, the **System.DateTime** structure and the **System.TimeSpan** structure. Both offer methods for parsing and formatting and differ only in the scope of data they can handle. This section explains the two structures. There is also the **System.Globalization.Calendar** class, which can manipulate dates and times, and its subclasses. However, I will limit discussion to **DateTime** and **TimeSpan** and will not be discussing **Calendar** and its next of kin.

System.DateTime

DateTime represents a point in time, like August 9, 1945 or 6.20pm on December 20, 2020.

For example, the **DayCalculator** class in Listing 9.3 shows how to parse and format a date using **DateTime**.

Listing 9.3: The DayCalculator class

```
using System;
using System.Globalization;

namespace App09
{
    class DayCalculator
    {
        public void CalculateDay()
        {
            Console.Write("\nEnter a date in MM/dd/yyyy format: ");
            DateTime selectedDate;
            string dateString = Console.ReadLine();
            string format = "MM/dd/yyyy";
            CultureInfo provider = CultureInfo.InvariantCulture;

            try
            {
                selectedDate = DateTime.ParseExact(dateString,
```

```
                    format, provider);
                Console.WriteLine("{0} is/was a {1}",
                    selectedDate.ToString("MMM dd, yyyy"),
                    selectedDate.DayOfWeek);

                DateTime now = DateTime.Now;
                // create DateTime with the same date this year
                DateTime thisYear = new DateTime(
                    now.Year, selectedDate.Month,
                    selectedDate.Day);

                Console.WriteLine("This year {0} falls/fell "
                    + "on a {1}",
                    thisYear.ToString("MMM dd"),
                    thisYear.DayOfWeek);
            }
            catch (FormatException) {
                Console.WriteLine("Invalid date. Note that the "
                    + "month and date parts must be two digits. "
                    + "For example, instead of 1/1/2011, "
                    + "enter 01/01/2011");
            }
        }

        static void Main(string[] args)
        {
            DayCalculator dayCalculator =
                new DayCalculator();
            char tryAgain = 'y';
            while (tryAgain != 'n' && tryAgain != 'N')
            {
                if (tryAgain == 'y' || tryAgain == 'Y')
                {
                    dayCalculator.CalculateDay();
                }
                Console.Write("\nTry again (y/n)?");
                tryAgain = Console.ReadKey().KeyChar;
            }
        }
    }
}
```

The **CalculateDay** method is the brain in **DayCalculator**. It takes user input, parses it, and prints the day of the entered date.

System.TimeSpan

The **TimeSpan** structure represents a time interval and can be used to hold a time information. Unlike **DateTime** that can be used to contain date and time information, **TimeSpan** can only hold time information and is therefore easier to use than **DateTime** if you don't need the date component.

For example, the **TimeSpanExample** project in **App09** solution shows how you can use **TimeSpan** to calculate how long a flight will take given the departure and arrival times. Only time information is needed as a flight in this example is assumed to start and end on the same day.

The **DurationCalculator** class is given in Listing 9.4.

Listing 9.4: The DurationCalculator class

```
using System;
using System.Globalization;

namespace TimeSpanExample
{
    class DurationCalculator
    {
        public void CalculateDuration()
        {
            TimeSpan departure,
            TimeSpan arrival;
            string format = "h\\:mm";
            bool timeValid = true;
            do
            {
                Console.Write("Departure time (hh:mm):");
                string intervalString = Console.ReadLine();
                timeValid = TimeSpan.TryParseExact(intervalString,
                    format, CultureInfo.CurrentCulture,
                    TimeSpanStyles.None, out departure);
                if (!timeValid)
                {
                    Console.WriteLine("Invalid time. Please "
                        + "enter your departure time in hh:mm "
                        + "format (Ex: 10:30 or 21:12)\n");
                }
            }
```

```
        while (!timeValid);

        do
        {
            Console.Write("Arrival time (hh:mm):");
            string intervalString = Console.ReadLine();
            timeValid = TimeSpan.TryParseExact(intervalString,
                format, CultureInfo.CurrentCulture,
                TimeSpanStyles.None, out arrival);
            if (!timeValid)
            {
                Console.WriteLine("Invalid time. Please "
                    + "enter your arrival time in hh:mm "
                    + "format (Ex: 10:30 or 21:12)\n");
            }
        }
        while (!timeValid);

        if (arrival.CompareTo(departure) > 0)
        {
            TimeSpan duration = arrival.Subtract(departure);
            Console.WriteLine("Your flight will take {0} "
                + "hour(s) and {1} minute(s)",
                duration.Hours, duration.Minutes);
        }
        else
        {
            Console.WriteLine("You have entered an arrival "
                + "time that is earlier than the departure "
                + "time.\nPlease try again later. ");
        }
    }

    static void Main(string[] args)
    {
        DurationCalculator calculator = new
            DurationCalculator();
        calculator.CalculateDuration();
        Console.ReadKey();
    }
    }
}
```

The **CalculateDuration** method in **DurationCalculator** does all the work. It employs two **do-while** loops that take the departure time and arrival time, respectively. In each loop, **CalculateDuration** invokes **Console.ReadLine()** to take user input and feed the input to the **TryParseExact** static method of **TimeSpan**. Here is the **do-while** loop for the departure time.

```
bool timeValid = true;
do
{
    Console.Write("Departure time (hh:mm):");
    string intervalString = Console.ReadLine();
    timeValid = TimeSpan.TryParseExact(intervalString,
        format, CultureInfo.CurrentCulture,
        TimeSpanStyles.None, out departure);
    if (!timeValid)
    {
        Console.WriteLine("Invalid time. Please "
            + "enter your departure time in hh:mm "
            + "format (Ex: 10:30 or 21:12)\n");
    }
}
while (!timeValid);
```

TryParseExact returns **true** if parsing was successful and **false** if parsing failed. The last argument of **TryParseExact** is an out argument, which means the **TimeSpan** object is set on successful parsing. Basically, the **do-while** loop will keep on looping until the user enters a valid time in hh:mm format.

The second **while** loop is similar to the first, except for the error message. After a valid arrival time is received, the arrival time is compared with the departure time.

```
if (arrival.CompareTo(departure) > 0)
{
    TimeSpan duration = arrival.Subtract(departure);
    Console.WriteLine("Your flight will take {0} "
        + "hour(s) and {1} minute(s)",
        duration.Hours, duration.Minutes);
}
else
{
```

```
                        Console.WriteLine("You have entered an arrival "
                            + "time that is earlier than the departure "
                            + "time.\nPlease try again later. ");
                }
```

arrival.CompareTo(departure) returns a positive integer if *arrival* is greater than *departure*. In such a case, departure will be subtracted from arrival and the result (duration) is printed. On the other hand, if *departure* is the same as or greater than arrival, **CalculateDuration** prints an error message.

Finally, here is the **Main** method that instantiates **DurationCalculator** and calls the **CalculateDuration** method.

```
        static void Main(string[] args)
        {
            DurationCalculator calculator = new
                DurationCalculator();
            calculator.CalculateDuration();
            Console.ReadKey();
        }
```

Running this program, you'll see this message on your console:

```
Departure time (HH:mm):
```

Enter a time, such as 10:00 and press Enter. You'll get a second message urging you to enter an arrival time.

```
Arrival time (HH:mm):
```

Enter a time, such as 12:00, and press Enter. You'll get the duration between the first and second time spans. Conversely, you'll get an error message if you type in an invalid time or if the arrival time is not greater than the departure time.

Summary

In C# numbers are represented by types such as **byte**, **short**, **int**, **float**, **double**, and **long**. These C# types are aliases for .NET structures **System.Byte**, **System.Int16**, **System.Int32**, **System.Single**,

System.Double, and **System.Int64**, respectively. In addition, dates are represented by the **System.DateTime** structure. In this chapter you learned the three issues that you need to address when working with numbers and dates: parsing, formatting, and manipulation.

Chapter 10
Interfaces and Abstract Classes

C# beginners often get the impression that an interface is simply a class without implementation code. While this is not technically incorrect, it obscures the real purpose of having the interface in the first place. The interface is more than that. The interface should be regarded as a contract between a service provider and its clients. This chapter therefore focuses on the concepts before explaining how to write an interface.

The second topic in this chapter is the abstract class. Technically speaking, an abstract class is a class that cannot be instantiated and must be implemented by a subclass. However, the abstract class is important because in some situations it can take the role of the interface. You'll see how to use the abstract class too in this chapter.

The Concept of Interface

When learning about the interface for the first time, novices often focus on how to write one, rather than understanding the concept behind it. They would think an interface is something like a class declared with the **interface** keyword and whose methods have no body.

While the description is not inaccurate, treating an interface as an implementation-less class misses the big picture. A better definition of an interface is a contract. It is a contract between a service provider (server) and the user of such a service (client). Sometimes the server defines the contract, sometimes the client does.

Consider this real-world example. Microsoft Windows is the most popular operating system today, but Microsoft does not make printers. For printing, we still rely on those people at HP, Canon, Samsung, and the like.

Each of these printer makers uses a proprietary technology. However, their products can all be used to print any document from any Windows application. How come?

This is because Microsoft said something to this effect to printer manufacturers, "If you want your products useable on Windows (and we know you all do), you must implement this **IPrintable** interface."

The interface is as simple as this:

```
interface IPrintable
{
    void Print(Document document);
}
```

where *document* is the document to be printed.

Implementing this interface, printer makers then write printer drivers. Every printer has a different driver, but they all implement **IPrintable**. A printer driver is an implementation of **IPrintable**. In this case, these printer drivers are the service provider.

The client of the printing service is all Windows applications. It is easy to print on Windows because an application just needs to call the **Print** method and pass a **Document** object. Because the interface is freely available, client applications can be compiled without waiting for an implementation to be available.

The point is, printing to different printers from different applications is possible thanks to the **IPrintable** interface. A contract between printing service providers and printing clients.

An interface can define methods and other members. However, methods in an interface have no implementation. To be useful, an interface has to have an implementation class that actually performs the action.

Figure 10.1 illustrates the **IPrintable** interface and its implementation in an UML class diagram.

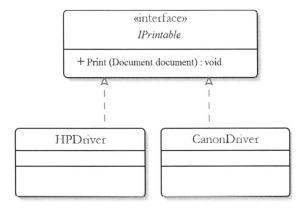

Figure 10.1: An interface and two implementation classes in a class diagram

In the class diagram, an interface has the same shape as a class, however the name is printed in italic and prefixed with <<interface>>. The **HPDriver** and **CanonDriver** classes implement the **IPrintable** interface. The implementations are of course different. In the **HPDriver** class, the **Print** method contains code that enables printing to a HP printer. In **CanonDriver**, the code enables printing to a Canon driver. In a UML class diagram, a class and an interface are joined by a dash-line with an arrow. This type of relationship is often called realization because the class provides real implementation (code that actually works) of the abstraction provided by the interface.

Note

This case study is contrived but the problem and the solution are real. I hope this provides you with more understanding of what the interface really is. It is a contract.

Another real-world example to illustrate this point is the **System.Data.IDbConnection** interface, which defines a contract for all data providers that facilitates connecting to different relational databases from C# codes. As long as a database maker provides an implementation of **IDbConnection**, their product will be accessible from any .NET application.

Note
IDbConnection is discussed in Chapter 17, "ADO.NET."

The Interface, Technically Speaking

Now that you understand what the interface is, let's examine how you can create one. In C#, like the class, the interface is a type. Follow this format to write an interface:

```
interface interfaceName
{

}
```

An interface may contain the signatures of methods, properties, events, and delegates. An interface may not contain the implementation of those members. In addition, an interface must not contain fields.

All interface members are implicitly public. By convention interface names are prefixed with **I**. You should follow this convention as it is a best practice to do so.

The interface is one of the most commonly used types and there are hundreds of them in the .NET Framework class library. Examples include **System.IClonable**, **System.IComparable**, **System.IFormatProvider**, **System.Collection.IList**, **System.Runtime.Serialization.ISerializable**, and **System.Data.IDbConnection**.

It is easy to write an interface. Listing 10.1 shows an interface named **IPrintable**.

Listing 10.1: The IPrintable interface

```
public interface IPrintable
{
    void Print(Object document);
}
```

The **IPrintable** interface defines one method, **Print**. Note that **Print** is public even though there is no **public** keyword in front of the method declaration. In fact, you cannot have an access modifier (such as **public** or

protected) in the method declaration in an interface. Note that only the signature of **Print** appears here. The implementation is written in the implementing class or structure.

Just like a class, an interface is a template for creating objects. Unlike an ordinary class, however, an interface cannot be instantiated. It simply defines a set of methods that C# classes can implement.

To implement an interface, you use the colon (:) after the class declaration. For example, Listing 10.2 shows a **CanonDriver** class that implements **IPrintable**.

Listing 10.2: An implementation of the IPrintable interface

```
public class CanonDriver : IPrintable
{
    public void Print(Object document)
    {
        // code that does the printing
    }
}
```

An implementation class has to override all methods in the interface. The relationship between an interface and its implementing class can be likened to a parent class and a subclass. An instance of the class is also an instance of the interface. For example, the following **if** statement evaluates to **true**.

```
CanonDriver driver = new CanonDriver();
if (driver is IPrintable)    // evaluates to true
```

A class may implement multiple interfaces. In the class definition, multiple interface names are separated by a comma. For example, this is the definition of a class that implements both **IPrintable** and **System.IComparable**:

```
public class MyPrinter : IPrintable, System.IComparable
```

Of course, if you implement multiple interfaces, you must provide implementations for all the methods in the interfaces.

You can also write a class that extends a base class and implements an interface. For instance, here is the definition of a class that extends **BasePrinter** and implements both **IPrintable** and **System.IComparable**.

```
public class MyPrinter : BasePrinter, IPrintable, System.IComparable
```

One thing to note if you're extending a class and implementing one or many interfaces is the name of the class you're extending must come before the names of the interfaces. For instance, the following declaration will generate a compile error:

```
public class MyPrinter : IPrintable, System.IComparable, BasePrinter
```

The interface supports inheritance. An interface can extend another interface. If interface **B** extends interface **A**, **B** is said to be a subinterface of **A**. **A** is the superinterface of **B**. Because **B** directly extends **A**, **A** is the direct superinterface of **B**. Any interface that extends **B** is an indirect subinterface of **A**. Figure 10.2 shows an interface that extends another interface. Note that the type of the line connecting both interfaces is the same as the one used for extending a class.

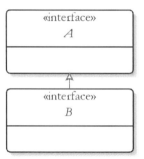

Figure 10.2: Extending an interface

Most of the time, you will define method members in an interface. You declare the signatures of methods in an interface just as you would in a class. However, methods in an interface do not have a body, they are immediately terminated by a semicolon. All methods are implicitly public and abstract, and it is illegal to have an access modifier in a method/property/event/delegate signature.

The syntax of a method in an interface is

```
ReturnType MethodName(listOfArgument);
```

Note that methods in an interface must not be declared static because static methods cannot be abstract.

Implementing System.IComparable

The following example shows the role of an interface as a contract between a service provider and a service user. The objective of this example is to make it easier for you to grasp the concept of interface in an OOP language.

You learned about arrays in Chapter 5, "Core Classes" and I cursorily mentioned that the **System.Array** class has a static method named **Sort** that can sort elements of an array. Its signature is as follows:

```
public static void Sort(Array array)
```

But how does **Sort** know how to sort objects that it knows nothing about? How does **Sort** know that **Elephant** objects should be sorted by weight and **Student** objects should be ordered by last name and first name? Well, this is where an interface comes into play. Since the author(s) of **System.Array** knew nothing about the objects, they simply drew a contract that says **Sort** will treat array elements as **System.IComparable** instances. So, if you want your objects in an array to be sortable, you have to allow them to be cast to **IComparable** by making sure the object class implements the interface.

IComparable only has one method, **CompareTo**, that you can override to determine how your objects can and should be sorted.

The **IComparableImplementation** project contains a class that is presented in Listing 10.3.

Listing 10.3: Implementing Icomparable

```
using System;

namespace App10
{
    class Student : IComparable
    {
        private string firstName;
        private string lastName;

        public Student(string firstName,
            string lastName)
        {
            this.lastName = lastName;
```

```
            this.firstName = firstName;
        }

        public string FirstName
        {
            get
            {
                return firstName;
            }
            set
            {
                firstName = value;
            }
        }

        public string LastName
        {
            get
            {
                return lastName;
            }
            set
            {
                lastName = value;
            }
        }

        public int CompareTo(Object obj)
        {
            Student anotherStudent = (Student) obj;
            if (this.lastName == anotherStudent.lastName)
            {
                return this.FirstName.CompareTo(
                    anotherStudent.FirstName);
            }
            else
            {
                return this.LastName.CompareTo(
                    anotherStudent.LastName);
            }
        }
    }

class Program
{
    static void Main(string[] args)
```

```
    {
        Student[] students = {
            new Student("John", "Suzuki"),
            new Student("Liam", "Doe"),
            new Student("John", "Smith"),
            new Student("Joe", "Doe"),
            new Student("John", "Tirano"),
            new Student("Louis", "Smith")};

        Console.WriteLine("\nUnsorted:");
        Console.WriteLine("====================");
        foreach (Student student in students)
        {
            Console.WriteLine(student.LastName +
                ", " + student.FirstName);
        }

        Array.Sort(students);

        Console.WriteLine("\nSorted:");
        Console.WriteLine("====================");
        foreach (Student student in students)
        {
            Console.WriteLine(student.LastName +
                ", " + student.FirstName);
        }

        Console.ReadKey();
    }
  }
}
```

Running the code in Listing 10.3 shows the following result on the console.

```
Unsorted:
====================
Suzuki, John
Doe, Liam
Smith, John
Doe, Joe
Tirano, John
Smith, Louis

Sorted:
====================
```

```
Doe, Joe
Doe, Liam
Smith, John
Smith, Louis
Suzuki, John
Tirano, John
```

Abstract Classes

With the interface, you have to write an implementation class that perform the actual action. If there are many methods in the interface, you risk wasting time overriding methods that you don't use. An abstract class has a similar role to an interface, i.e. provide a contract between a service provider and its clients, but at the same time an abstract class can provide partial implementation. Methods that must be explicitly overridden can be declared abstract. You still need to create an implementation class because you cannot instantiate an abstract class, but you don't need to override methods you don't want to use or change.

You create an abstract class by using the **abstract** modifier in the class declaration. To create an abstract method, use the **abstract** modifier in front of the method declaration. Listing 10.4 shows an abstract **DefaultPrinter** class as an example.

Listing 10.4: The DefaultPrinter class

```
public abstract class DefaultPrinter
{
    public string GetDescription()
    {
        return "Use this to print documents.";
    }
    public abstract void Print(Object document);
}
```

There are two methods in **DefaultPrinter**, **Print** and **GetDescription**. The **GetDescription** method has an implementation, so you do not need to override this method in an implementation class, unless you want to change its return value. The **Print** method is declared abstract and does not have a body. Listing 10.5 presents a **MyPrinterClass** class that is the implementation class of **DefaultPrinter**.

Listing 10.5: An implementation of DefaultPrinter

```
public class MyPrinter : DefaultPrinter
{
    public override void Print(object document)
    {
        Console.WriteLine("Printing document");
        // some code here
    }
}
```

A concrete implementation class such as **MyPrinter** must override all abstract methods. Otherwise, it itself must be declared abstract.

Declaring a class abstract is a way to tell the class user that you want them to extend the class. You can still declare a class abstract even if it does not have an abstract method.

In UML class diagrams, an abstract class looks similar to a concrete class, except that the name is italicized. Figure 10.3 shows an abstract class.

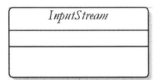

Figure 10.3: An abstract class

Summary

The interface plays an important role in C# because it defines a contract between a service provider and its clients. This chapter showed you how to use the interface. A base class provides a generic implementation of an interface and expedites program development by providing default implementation of code.

An abstract class is like an interface, but it may provide implementation of some of its methods.

Chapter 11
Enumerations

Enums are a data type in .NET Framework that can be used to hold enumerated values. You primarily use enums to restrict the possible values that can be assigned to a variable or returned from a method.

This chapter shines a light on this data type.

An Overview of Enum

You use the keyword **enum** to create a set of valid values for a field or a method. For example, the only possible values for the **customerType** field may be **Individual** and **Organization**. For the **state** field, valid values may be all the states in the US plus Canadian provinces. With **enum**, you can easily restrict your program to take only one of the valid values.

An enum type can stand alone or can be part of a class. You make it stand alone if it needs to be used in many places in your application. If it is only used from inside a class, the enum is better made part of the class.

As an example, consider the **EmployeeType** enum definition in Listing 11.1.

Listing 11.1: The EmployeeType enum

```
enum EmployeeType
{
    FullTime,
    PartTime,
    Permanent,
    Contractor
}
```

The **EmployeeType** enum has four enumerated values: **FullTime**, **PartTime**, **Permanent**, and **Contractor**. Enum values are case sensitive and by convention capitalized. Two enum values are separated by a comma and values can be written on a single line or multiple lines. The enum in Listing 11.1 is written in multiple lines to improve readability.

Using an enum is like using a class or an interface. For example, the code in Listing 11.2 uses the **EmployeeType** enum in Listing 11.1 as a field type.

Listing 11.2: Using the EmployeeType Enum

```
using System;
namespace EnumExample
{
    enum EmployeeType
    {
        FullTime,
        PartTime,
        Permanent,
        Contractor
    }

    class Employee
    {
        private EmployeeType employeeType;
        public Employee(EmployeeType employeeType)
        {
            this.employeeType = employeeType;
        }
        public String getDescription()
        {
            if (employeeType == EmployeeType.Contractor)
            {
                return "Contractor, pay on hourly basis";
            }
            else if (employeeType == EmployeeType.FullTime)
            {
                return "Permanent, salary-based";
            }
            else if (employeeType == EmployeeType.PartTime)
            {
                return "Part-Time, mostly students";
            }
            else
```

```
            {
                return "Full-Time, salary-based";
            }
        }
    }
    class Program
    {
        static void Main(string[] args)
        {
            EmployeeType employeeType = EmployeeType.PartTime;
            Employee employee = new Employee(employeeType);
            Console.WriteLine(employeeType); // prints "PartTime"
            Console.WriteLine(employee.getDescription());
            Console.ReadKey();
        }
    }
}
```

In Listing 11.2, you use a value in an enum just like you would a class's static member. For example, this code illustrates the use of **EmployeeType**.

```
EmployeeType employeeType = EmployeeType.PartTime;
```

Notice how the **employeeType** variable is assigned the enumerated value **PartTime** of the **EmployeeType** enum? Because the **employeeType** variable is of type **EmployeeType**, it can only be assigned a value defined in **EmployeeType**.

The use of **enum** at first glance is no difference than the use of constants. However, there are some basic differences between enums and constants. Constants are not a perfect solution for something that should accept only predefined values. For example, consider the **CustomerTypeStaticFinals** class in Listing 11.3.

Listing 11.3: Using constants

```
class CustomerTypeStaticFinals
{
    public const int INDIVIDUAL = 1;
    public const int ORGANIZATION = 2;
}
```

Suppose you have a class named **OldFashionedCustomer** that uses an **int** for its **customerType** field. The following code creates an instance of **OldFashionedCustomer** and assigns a value to its **customerType** field:

```
OldFashionedCustomer ofCustomer = new OldFashionedCustomer();
ofCustomer.customerType = 5;
```

With constants there is nothing preventing you from assigning an invalid integer to **customerType**. To guarantee that a variable is assigned only a valid value, enums are better than constants.

Enums in a Class

You can use enums as members of a class. You use this approach if the enum is only used internally inside the class. For example, the code in Listing 11.4 is a modified version of the one in Listing 11.3. Unlike in Listing 11.3, the code in Listing 11.4 declares the **EmployeeType** enum as a field in the **Employee** class.

Listing 11.4: Using an enum as a class member

```
using System;

namespace EnumExample2
{
    class Employee
    {
        public enum EmployeeType
        {
            FullTime,
            PartTime,
            Permanent,
            Contractor
        }
        private EmployeeType employeeType;
        public Employee(EmployeeType employeeType)
        {
            this.employeeType = employeeType;
        }
        public String getDescription()
        {
            if (employeeType == EmployeeType.Contractor)
```

```
        {
            return "Contractor, pay on hourly basis";
        }
        else if (employeeType == EmployeeType.Permanent)
        {
            return "Permanent, salary-based";
        }
        else if (employeeType == EmployeeType.PartTime)
        {
            return "Part-Time, mostly students";
        }
        else
        {
            return "Full-Time, salary-based";
        }
    }
}
class Program
{
    static void Main(string[] args)
    {
        Employee.EmployeeType employeeType =
                Employee.EmployeeType.FullTime;
        Employee employee = new Employee(employeeType);
        Console.WriteLine(employeeType); // prints "FullTime"
        Console.WriteLine(employee.getDescription());
        Console.ReadKey();
    }
}
}
```

Switching on enum

The **switch** statement can also work on enumerated values of an enum. The code in Listing 11.5 is an example of using an enum, **DayOfWeek**, in a switch statement.

Listing 11.5: Switching on enum

```
using System;

namespace EnumExample3
{
```

```
enum DayOfWeek
{
    Monday, Tuesday, Wednesday, Thursday, Friday, Saturday,
        Sunday
}

class Program
{
    static void Main(string[] args)
    {
        DayOfWeek day = DayOfWeek.Sunday;
        switch (day)
        {
            case DayOfWeek.Monday:
            case DayOfWeek.Tuesday:
            case DayOfWeek.Wednesday:
            case DayOfWeek.Thursday:
            case DayOfWeek.Friday:
                Console.WriteLine("Week day");
                break;
            case DayOfWeek.Saturday:
            case DayOfWeek.Sunday:
                Console.WriteLine("Week end");
                break;
        }
        Console.ReadKey();
    }
}
```

The **switch** statement in Listing 11.5 accepts a value in **DayOfWeek**. It will print "Week day" if the value is Monday, Tuesday, Wednesday, Thursday, or Friday. It will print "Week end" if the value is Saturday or Sunday.

Summary

C# supports enum, a special class that is a subclass of **System.Enum**. Enums are preferred over integers because they are more secure. You can also switch on an enum and iterate its values.

Chapter 12
Generics

Generics were one of the most prominent features added to .NET Framework 2.0. With generics you can write a parameterized type and create instances of it by passing a type or types. The objects will then be restricted to the type(s). In addition to parameterized types, generics support parameterized methods.

The benefit of generics include stricter type checking at compile time and performance improvement. In addition, generics eliminate most type castings you would otherwise have to perform when working with members of the **System.Collections** namespace.

This chapter explains how you can use and write generic types. It starts with the section "Why Generics?" and then presents some examples of generic types. After a discussion of the syntax, this chapter concludes with a section that explains how to write generic types.

Why Generics?

It is easiest to argue for the case of generics with an example. Consider the **System.Collections.ArrayList** class that has been in the .NET Framework since version 1.0. **ArrayList** is a collection that can hold objects. To add an object to an **ArrayList**, you call its **Add** method. The method has the following signature.

```
public virtual int Add(Object value)
```

For example, the following code instantiates **ArrayList** and adds a product code (a string) to it.

```
ArrayList productCodes = new ArrayList();
```

```
codes.Add("ABC");
```

Since all reference and value types derive from **System.Object**, effectively you can pass any type of object to **ArrayList.Add**. The design is intentional as **ArrayList** should act as a general-purpose container that can hold any type of object.

After you store objects in an **ArrayList**, you can retrieve an element just as you would an array element.

arrayList[index]

Be aware that the return value will be of type **Object**, and you need to downcast it in order to fully use it. Modifying the code above:

```
ArrayList productCodes = new ArrayList();
codes.Add("ABC");
// retrieve the first element
string productCode = (string) productCodes[0];
```

Having to downcast from object to the actual object type is a bit of inconvenience, but you can probably live with it. On the other hand, consider the following code, which has more dire consequences:

```
int x = 123;
ArrayList productCodes = new ArrayList();
productCodes.Add("ABC");
productCodes.Add(x);
```

You're passing two different types here, a string ("ABC") and an int (*x*). Now, suppose you then try to iterate over the **ArrayList**, thinking that all objects in it are strings.

```
int count = codes.Count;
for (int i = 0; i < count; i++)
{
    // print in uppercase
    string code = (string)codes[i];
    Console.WriteLine(code.ToUpper());
}
```

What do you think will happen? It will crash on the second element as the type is **int** and trying to cast an **int** to string results in a runtime error.

So **ArrayList** is not cool as the flaw can be fatal.

Realizing this imperfection, the designers of .NET added generics in .NET 2.0. As a result, there is now a namespace called **System.Collections.Generic**.

Take **System.Collections.Generic.List**, for example. This class is very similar to **System.Collections.ArrayList**, except that **List** is parameterized. Here is the class declaration of **List**.

```
public class List<T> : IList<T>, ICollection<T>,
    IEnumerable<T>, IList, ICollection, IEnumerable
```

Here, **T** represents a type, the type of objects that it can store. To instantiate **List**, you must specify a type, such as **int** or **string**. For example, here is how you would declare a **List** of strings:

```
List<string> codes = new List<string>();
```

What this means is, you can only add strings to **codes**. Adding a type other than string would generate a compile error.

```
List<string> codes = new List<string>();
codes.Add("ABC");
codes.Add(123); // compile error
```

In other words, you cannot make a mistake of passing two different object types to a **List**. On top of that, since **List** can only accept a specific type, you don't need to downcast elements you retrieve. Here is a code snippet that shows that.

```
List<string> codes = new List<string>();
codes.Add("ABC");

// add more elements here

// iterate over List
int count = codes.Count;
for (int i = 0; i < count; i++)
{
    // print in uppercase
    string code = codes[i]; // no downcasting
    Console.WriteLine(code.ToUpper());
}
```

You'll see more members of **System.Collections.Generic** in action in Chapter 13. For now, let's find out more about generics.

Introducing Generic Types

As shown in the previous section, a generic type can accept parameters. This is why a generic type is often called a parameterized type.

Declaring a generic type is like declaring a non-generic one, except that you use angle brackets to enclose the list of type variables for the generic type.

```
MyType<typeVar1, typeVar2, ...>
```

For example, to declare a **System.Collections.Generic.List**, you would write so.

```
List<T> myList;
```

T is called a type variable, namely a variable that will be replaced by a type. The value substituting for a type variable will then be used as the argument type or the return type of a method or methods in the generic type. For the **List** class, when an instance is created, **T** will be used as the argument type of **Add** and other methods. **T** will also be used as the return type of **Find** and other methods. Here are the signatures of **Add** and **Find** in the **List** class.

```
public void Add<T item>
```

```
public T Find(Predicate<T> match)
```

Note
A generic type that uses a type variable **T** allows you to pass **T** when declaring or instantiating the generic type. Additionally, if **T** is a class, you may also pass a subclass of **T**; if **T** is an interface, you may pass a class that implements **T**.

If you pass **string** to a declaration of **List**, as in

```
List<string> myList;
```

the **Add** method of the **List** instance referenced by **myList** will expect a **string** object as its argument and its **Find** method will return a **string**. Because **Find** returns a specific type of object, no downcasting is required.

To instantiate a generic type, you pass the same list of parameters as when declaring it. For instance, to create a **List** that works with **string**, you pass **string** in angle brackets.

```
List<string> myList = new List<string>();
```

As an example, Listing 12.1 compares **ArrayList** and **List**.

Listing 12.1: Comparing non-generic ArrayList and generic List

```
using System;
using System.Collections;
using System.Collections.Generic;

namespace ArrayListVsList
{
    class Program
    {
        static void Main(string[] args)
        {
            ArrayList arrayList = new ArrayList();
            arrayList.Add("Life without generics");
            // cast to String
            String s1 = (String) arrayList[0];
            Console.WriteLine(s1.ToUpper());

            List<string> list = new List<string>();
            list.Add("Life with generics");
            // no type casting necessary
            String s2 = list[0];
            Console.WriteLine(s2.ToUpper());


            Console.ReadKey();
        }
    }
}
```

In Listing 12.1, **ArrayList** is compared head-to-head with **List**. The declaration **List<string>** tells the compiler that this instance of **List** can only store **string**s. When retrieving member elements of the **List**, no downcasting is necessary because it already returns the intended type, namely **string**.

If you run the code in Listing 12.1, you'll see these lines on the console:

```
LIFE WITHOUT GENERICS
LIFE WITH GENERICS
```

Note
With generic types, type checking is done at compile time.

What's interesting here is the fact that a generic type is itself a type and can be used as a type variable. For example, if you want a **List** to store lists of strings, you can declare the **List** by passing **List<string>** as its type variable, as in

```
List<List<string>> myListOfListsOfStrings;
```

To retrieve the first string from the first list in **myList**, you would write:

```
string s = myListOfListsOfStrings[0][0];
```

Listing 12.2 presents a class that uses a **List** that accepts a **List** of **string**s.

Listing 12.2: Working with List of Lists

```
using System;
using System.Collections.Generic;

namespace ListOfLists
{
    class Program
    {
        static void Main(string[] args)
        {
            List<string> listOfStrings = new List<string>();
            listOfStrings.Add("Hello again");
            List<List<string>> listOfLists =
                    new List<List<string>>();
            listOfLists.Add(listOfStrings);
            string s = listOfLists[0][0];
            Console.WriteLine(s); // prints "Hello again"
            Console.ReadKey();
        }
    }
}
```

Additionally, a generic type can accept more than one type argument. For example, the **System.Collections.Generic.Dictionary** class, which you can use to store key/value pairs, is defined as follows.

```
Public class Dictionary<TKey, TValue> : ...
```

TKey is used to denote the type of keys and **TValue** the type of values. The **Add** method of the **Dictionary** class has the following signature:

```
public void Add(TKey key, TValue value)
```

Listing 12.3 presents an example that uses a **Dictionary**.

Listing 12.3: Using the generic Dictionary

```
using System;
using System.Collections.Generic;

namespace DictionaryExample
{
    class Program
    {
        static void Main(string[] args)
        {
            Dictionary<int, string> flowers =
                    new Dictionary<int, string>();
            flowers.Add(1001, "Lily");
            flowers.Add(1002, "Rose");
            flowers.Add(1003, "Lotus");

            string favorite = flowers[1002];
            Console.WriteLine(favorite);

            Console.ReadKey();
        }
    }
}
```

In Listing 12.3, you created a **Dictionary** that had **int** as its key type and **string** as its value type. A retrieved value would always be of type **string**, even without type casting.

Applying Restrictions

As you have seen in previous sections, the **List** and **Dictionary** classes allow any type to be passed as the type argument(s). However, you can also restrict the type that can be used with a parameterized type. For example, if you have a **MathUtility** class that offers methods for handling mathematical operations, it does make sense to restrict the type argument of **MathUtility** to value types that represent numbers.

Table 12.1 shows the constraints that can be used for type arguments.

Constraint	Description
where T: struct	The type argument must be a value type
where T: class	The type argument must be a reference type, including any class, interface, delegate, and array type.
where T: new()	The type argument must have a no-argument public constructor. If this constraint must appear last if there are other constraints.
where T: <base class name>	The type argument must be the specified base class or a child class of it.
where T: <interface name>	The type argument must be the specified interface or a type implementing it.
where T: U	The type argument for T must be the same as the argument for U or derive from it.

Table 12.1: Constraints for type arguments

For example, to restrict the type parameter to value types, use the **where T: struct** constraint.

```
Class MathUtility<T> where T: struct
{
}
```

If you try to pass a reference type to **MathUtility**, you'll get a compile error telling you that the type argument must be a value type.

As another example, the following class expects a type argument that implements **IComparable**:

```
class ObjecUtil<T> where T: Icomparable
{
}
```

Writing Generic Types

Writing a generic type is not much different from writing other types, except for the fact that you declare a list of type variables that you intend to use somewhere in your type. These type variables come in angle brackets after the type name. For example, the **Point** class in Listing 12.4 is a generic class. A **Point** object represents a point in a coordinate system and has an X component (abscissa) and a Y component (ordinate). By making **Point** generic, you can specify the degree of accuracy of a **Point** instance. For example, if a **Point** object needs to be very accurate, you can pass **Double** as the type variable. Otherwise, **Integer** would suffice.

Listing 12.4: The generic Point class

```
using System;

namespace CustomGenericType
{
    struct Point<T>
    {
        T x;
        T y;
        public Point(T x, T y)
        {
            this.x = x;
            this.y = y;
        }
        public T X
        {
            get { return x; }
            set { this.x = value; }
        }

        public T Y
        {
            get { return y; }
            set { this.y = value; }
```

```
        }

        public void Print()
        {
            Console.WriteLine("({0}, {1})", x, y);
        }
    }
}
```

In Listing 12.4, **T** is the type variable for the **Point** class. **T** is used as the return value and argument type for the **X** and **Y** properties. In addition, the constructor also accepts two **T** type variables.

Using **Point** is just like using other generic types. For example, the code in Listing 12.5 creates two **Point** objects, **point1** and **point2**. The former passes **Integer** as the type variable, the latter **Double**.

Listing 12.5: Testing Point

```
using System;

namespace CustomGenericType
{
    class Program
    {
        static void Main(string[] args)
        {
            Point<int> a = new Point<int>();
            a.Print();
            Point<double> b = new Point<double>(12.3, 244.4);
            b.Print();

            Console.ReadKey();
        }
    }
}
```

If you run the program, you'll see this on the console:

```
(0, 0)
(12.3, 244.4)
```

Summary

Generics enable stricter type checking at compile time. Used especially with members of the **System.Collections.Generic** namespace, generics make two contributions. First, they add type checking to collection types at compile time, so that the object type that a collection can hold is restricted to the type passed to it. For example, you can now create an instance of **System.Collections.Generic.List** that hold strings and will not accept **Integer** or other types. Second, generics eliminate the need for type casting when retrieving an element from a collection.

In this chapter you have also learned that passing different type variables to a generic type results in different types. This is to say that **List<String>** is a different type than **List<Object>**. Even though **System.String** is a subclass of **System.Object**, passing a **List<String>** to a method that expects a **List<Object>** generates a compile error.

Finally, you have seen that writing generic types is not that different from writing ordinary C# types. You just need to declare a list of type variables in angle brackets after the type name. You then use these type variables as the types of method return values or as the types of method arguments.

Chapter 13
Collections

When writing an object-oriented program, you often work with groups of objects. In Chapter 5, "Core Classes" you learned that arrays can be used to group objects and iterate over elements. Unfortunately, arrays lack the flexibility you need to rapidly develop applications. For one, they cannot be resized. Fortunately, the .NET Framework comes with a set of interfaces and classes that make working with groups of objects easier. These interfaces and classes are part of the **System.Collections** namespace and its subnamespaces. **System.Collections** contains non-generic types that more or less have been replaced by the generic types in the **System.Collections.Generic** namespace. This chapter discusses the most frequently used types in **System.Collections.Generic**.

Overview

A collection is an object that groups other objects. Also referred to as a container, a collection provides methods to store, retrieve, and manipulate its elements. Collections help C# programmers manage objects easily.

A C# programmer should be familiar with the most important types in the **System.Collections.Generic** namespace. There are dozens of classes, structures, and interfaces in this namespace, and, due to space constraint, only the more important ones will be discussed here: **List**, **HashSet**, **Queue**, and **Dictionary**.

List, **HashSet**, and **Queue** are similar, they all are used for storing objects of the same type. **Dictionary** is good for storing key/value pairs. These types are discussed in the sections to come.

The List Class

A **List** is similar to an array but with more flexibility. When you create an array, you have to specify a size that cannot be changed. With a **List**, specifying a size is optional. As you add elements to a **List**, its capacity grows automatically if there's no more room for new elements.

List is a generic class, as such you need to tell the compiler what kind of object you want to store in it. Here is how you create a List of strings:

```
List<string> animals = new List<string>();
```

Or, if you feel you need to, you can specify a size for your **List**. Here is how you specify an initial capacity of 10.

```
List<string> animals = new List<String>(10);
```

In both cases, **List** will add its capacity automatically if you add more elements than the existing capacity. However, if you know beforehand how many elements you will store in a **List**, it's a good idea to specify an initial capacity to the maximum number of elements. This way, you will avoid time that needs to be spent for resizing the **List**.

The most frequently used operations you would do on a **List** is add an element, retrieve an element, find out how many elements are on it, and iterate over its elements.

To add an element to a **List**, call its **Add** method. To inquire how many objects there are in a **List**, call its **Count** property. Note that **Count** is different from the **Capacity** property. **Capacity** tells you the capacity of the **List**. You rarely have to know about the capacity of a **List** at a given time as it can increase automatically.

To retrieve an element from a **List**, use its **Item** property. Recall that you invoke this property by passing an index to the **List** variable as if it was an array, like this:

```
myList[0]
```

The first element is represented by index 0, the second by 1, and so on.

Finally, to iterate over all elements in a **List**, use the **foreach** loop.

```
foreach (T element in myList)
{
    // do something with element
}
```

You'll learn more about these methods and properties in the example later in this section.

More Important Methods

The following are some of the more important methods in List.

```
public void Add(T item)
```
Adds a new object to the **List**. The added item may be null and will be placed at the end of the list. Compare this to the **Insert** method.

```
public void Clear()
```
Removes all elements from the **List** and sets the **Count** property to 0.

```
public bool Contains(T item)
```
Inquires if an item is on the **List** and returns true if it is. Otherwise, returns false.

```
public T Find(Predicate<T> match)
```
Searches the **List** and returns the first element that matches the specified condition.

```
public void Insert(int index, T item)
```
Adds an item at the specified index.

```
public bool Remove(T item)
```
Removes the specified item from the **List**. It returns true if the item is successfully removed. Otherwise, it returns false.

```
public void RemoveAt(int index)
```
Removes the item at the specified index. Passing 0 to this method removes the first item in the list.

```
public void Sort()
```
Sorts the **List** using the default comparer.

```
public T[] ToArray()
```
Returns the elements as an array.

List Example

Listing 13.1 shows an example of **List** to store strings and iterate them using **foreach**.

Listing 13.1: An example of List

```
namespace ListExamples
{
    class Program
    {
        static void Main(string[] args)
        {
            List<string> titles = new List<string>();
            titles.Add("No Sun No Moon");
            titles.Add("The Desert Story");
            titles.Add("Belle!");

            string selectedTitle = titles[1];
            Console.WriteLine("Selected: " + selectedTitle);
            Console.WriteLine();


            foreach (string title in titles)
            {
                Console.WriteLine("title: " + title);
            }

            Console.ReadKey();
        }
    }
}
```

The result of running this class is given below.

```
Selected: The Desert Story

title: No Sun No Moon
title: The Desert Story
title: Belle!
```

The HashSet Class

A set is a data structure that can store values with no particular order and does not allow duplicates. A hash set is a set that is implemented using a hash table (a set can be implemented in some other ways). The term hash refers to a function used to compute an index of an element so that the element can be retrieved quickly.

In the .NET Framework, the **HashSet** class represents a hash set. **HashSet** is similar to **List**, there are **Add** and **Clear** methods that work like the **Add** and **Clear** methods in **List** and there is a **Count** property that returns the number of elements in the **HashSet**. Unlike **List**, however, **HashSet** does not allow duplicates. On top of that you cannot add or remove an item at a specific index. There is not even an **Item** to let you retrieve an element at a specified position.

On the other hand, **HashSet** provides methods that are useful for working with sets, such as **IsSubsetOf** and **IsSuperSetOf**.

Useful Methods

The following are some of the more important methods in **HashSet**.

```
public bool Add(T item)
```
Adds a new object to the **HashSet**. If the item added is already in the **HashSet**, it won't be added again and the method will return false.

```
public void Clear()
```
Removes all elements from the **HashSet** and sets the **Count** property to 0.

```
public bool Contains(T item)
```
Determines if an item is in the **HashSet** and returns true if it is. Otherwise, returns false.

```
public bool IsSubsetOf(IEnumerable other)
```
Determines if the **HashSet** is a subset of the specified collection.

```
public bool IsSupersetOf(IEnumerable other)
```
Determines if the **HashSet** is a superset of the specified collection.

HashSet Example

The code in Listing 13.2 shows how to use a **HashSet** to add strings. Find out what the **Add** method returns when you try to add a duplicate to it.

Listing 13.2: An example of HashSet

```
using System;
using System.Collections.Generic;

using System;
using System.Collections.Generic;

namespace HashSetExamples
{
    class Program
    {
        static void Main(string[] args)
        {
            HashSet<string> productCodes = new HashSet<string>();
            bool added = productCodes.Add("1234");
            Console.WriteLine("1234 added? " + added);

            // duplicate, this won't be added
            added = productCodes.Add("1234");
            Console.WriteLine("1234 added? " + added);
            added = productCodes.Add("999");
            Console.WriteLine("999 added? " + added);

            Console.WriteLine("\nProduct Codes:");
            foreach (string productCode in productCodes)
            {
                Console.WriteLine("product code: " + productCode);
            }
            Console.ReadKey();
        }
    }
}
```

Running the program will display this on the console.

```
1234 added? True
```

```
1234 added? False
999 added? True

Product Codes:
product code: 1234
product code: 999
```

The Queue Class

A **Queue** is a collection like a **List** and **HashSet**. What makes the **Queue** stand out is the fact that you can retrieve an element and remove it at the same time using the **Dequeue** method. To retrieve an element without removing it from the **Queue**, use the **Peek** method.

When you add an element to a **Queue**, by calling its **Enqueue** method, the element is added to the end of the queue. When you call **Dequeue** or **Peek**, you get an element from the beginning of the queue. Therefore, the **Queue** is a first-in-first-out (FIFO) system.

Useful Methods

Here are some of the more important methods defined in Queue.

`public void Enqueue(T item)`

Adds a new element to the end of the **Queue**. The element added can be null.

`public void Clear()`

Removes all elements from the **Queue** and sets its **Count** property to 0.

`public bool Contains(T item)`

Determines if an item is in the **Queue** and returns true if it is. Otherwise, returns false.

`public T Dequeue()`

Returns the element from the beginning of the **Queue** and removes it from the **Queue**.

`public T Peek()`

Returns the element from the beginning of the **Queue** without removing it from the **Queue**.

Queue Example

As an example, consider the code in Listing 13.3 that uses a **Queue** to add string elements.

Listing 13.3: An example of Queue

```
using System;
using System.Collections.Generic;

namespace QueueExamples
{
    class Program
    {
        static void Main(string[] args)
        {
            // Queue test
            Queue<string> cities = new Queue<string>();
            cities.Enqueue("Ottawa");
            cities.Enqueue("Ottawa");
            cities.Enqueue("Helsinki");

            foreach (string city in cities)
            {
                Console.WriteLine("city: " + city);
            }

            while (cities.Count > 0)
            {
                Console.WriteLine("selected: " + cities.Dequeue());
            }

            Console.ReadKey();

        }
    }
}
```

The following message is shown on the console upon running the program.

```
city: Ottawa
city: Ottawa
```

```
city: Helsinki
selected: Ottawa
selected: Ottawa
selected: Helsinki
```

The Dictionary Class

The **Dictionary** class is a template for creating containers that take key/value pairs. The **Dictionary** is suitable for storing elements that each consists of a key and a value, such as an ISBN and a **Book** object or a country and a capital.

To construct a **Dictionary**, you pass the type of the key and the type of the value to its constructor. For example, the following code snippet creates a **Dictionary** that takes a string as key and a **Book** object as value.

```
Dictionary books = new Dictionary(string, Book);
```

Like other types of collections, you have an **Add** method to add a key/value pair to a **Dictionary** and a **Clear** method to remove all its elements.

To retrieve a value, use its **Item** property. For example, if a **Dictionary** contains a country/capital pairs, use this syntax to retrieve a value:

```
string selectedCountry = countryDictionary[countryName];
```

Dictionary Example

As an example, consider the code in Listing 13.4 that shows off a **Dictionary** for storing country/capital pairs.

Listing 13.4: Dictionary Example

```
using System;
using System.Collections.Generic;

namespace DictionaryExamples
{
    class Program
    {
        static void Main(string[] args)
```

```
        {
                Dictionary<string, string> capitals =
                        new Dictionary<string, string>();
                capitals.Add("France", "Paris");
                capitals.Add("Australia", "Canberra");
                capitals.Add("Canada", "Ottawa");

                Console.WriteLine(capitals["Canada"]);
                // prints "Ottawa"

                Console.ReadKey();
        }
    }
}
```

Running the program in Listing 13.4 gives you this output.

```
Ottawa
```

Summary

Collections are good for working with groups of objects. The .NET Framework class library provides many of collection types that you can easily use. Version 1.0 of the .NET Framework featured collection types in the **System.Collections** namespace. As .NET 2.0 added generics as a feature, it also brought with it parameterized collection types, which can be found in the **System.Collections.Generic** namespace. You should always use the members of **System.Collections.Generic** instead of those in **System.Collections**. In this chapter you learned the four most important members of the **System.Collections.Generic** namespace, **List**, **HashSet**, **Queue**, and **Dictionary**.

Chapter 14
Input/Output

Input/output (I/O) is one of the most common operations performed by computer programs. Examples of I/O operations include

- creating and deleting files
- reading from and writing to a file or network socket
- serializing (or saving) objects to persistent storage and retrieving the saved objects

Support for I/O has been available since .NET Framework 1.0 in the form of the **System.IO** namespace and its subnamespaces. This chapter presents topics based on functionality and selects the most important members of **System.IO** namespace.

File and directory handling and manipulation are the first topic in this chapter. Here you learn how to create and delete files and directories as well as manipulate their attributes. Next, you learn what a stream is and how to use it in the section "Input/Output Streams." A stream acts like a water pipe that facilitates data transmission. Reading from and writing to a stream dictate that you do so sequentially, which means to read the second unit of data, you must read the first one first. There are several types of streams. **FileStream**, **NetworkStream**, and **MemoryStream** are some examples of streams. To make lives easier, there are utility classes for manipulating these streams so you don't have to use them directly. We take a look at these utility classes too.

File and Directory Handling and Manipulation

The .NET Framework class library comes with the **File** and **Directory** classes for creating and deleting files and directories, respectively. In addition, with **File** and **Directory** you can manipulate a file or directory, such as checking if a file/directory exists. In addition, there is also a **FileSystemInfo** class that is the parent class for **FileInfo** and **DirectoryInfo**. **FileInfo** offers much of the functionality in **File** and **DirectoryInfo** provides methods that do what **Directory**'s methods can do. It is sometimes confusing for a beginner to choose which one to use.

The following subsections elaborate what you can do with **File** and **Directory**.

Creating and Deleting A File

To create a file you use the **Create** method of **System.IO.File**. Here is its signature.

```
public static FileStream Create(string path)
```

For example, the following snippet creates a file and assigns it to a **FileStream**:

```
string fileName = @"C:\users\jayden\wintemp.txt";
try
{
    FileStream fs = File.Create(fileName);
}
catch (IOException e)
{
    Console.WriteLine(e.Message);
}
finally
{
    // call fs.Close() here
}
```

If the file to be created already exists, the **Create** method will overwrite the file with a new file. Also, most of the time, you'll need to put **File.Create** in a **try** block as it will throw an **IOException** if the operation fails, for example if you don't have permissions to create files in the specified directory.

A more convenient syntax for working with **File** is to use the **using** statement like this:

```
using (FileStream fs = File.Create(fileName))
{
    // do something with the FileStream here
}
```

With this syntax you don't have to worry about closing it as the **using** statement will take care of it. However, the **Create** method may throw an exception if it fails to create the file. As such, even when using the **using** statement, you still need to enclose your code in a **try** block like this:

```
try
{
    using (FileStream fs = File.Create(fileName))
    {
        // do something with the FileStream here
    }
}
catch (Exception e)
{
    // handle exception
}
```

Creating and Deleting A Directory

The **System.IO.Directory** class offers static methods for creating and deleting a directory and a subdirectory. To create a directory, use the **CreateDirectory** method.

```
public static DirectoryInfo CreateDirectory(string path)
```

CreateDirectory returns a **DirectoryInfo** that exposes a number of directory attributes, such as the creation time, the last access time, and so on. In addition, the **DirectoryInfo** class offer methods for retrieving and manipulating the files in the current directory. You will learn more about the **DirectoryInfo** class in the section "Working with File and Directory Attributes" later in this chapter.

CreateDirectory may throw an exception if the operation didn't complete successfully. For instance, if there was insufficient permission to carry out the task, the method will throw an

UnauthorizedAccessException. Likewise, trying to create a directory with the same path as an existing file will throw an **IOException**.

To delete a directory, use the **Delete** method of the **Directory** class. There are two overloads for this method:

```
public static void Delete(string path)
public static void Delete(string path, boolean recursive)
```

With the first overload, the directory must be writable and empty. Trying to delete a directory that is not empty will throw an **IOException**. Using the second overload, however, you can delete a non-empty directory if you pass true as the second argument. Note that the second overload will fail if the directory contains a read-only file.

Working with File and Directory Attributes

The **FileInfo** and **DirectoryInfo** classes are used for working with files and directories, respectively. With **FileInfo**, you can create and delete a file, even though the code would be less brief than if you're using the **File** class. Here is how to create a file with **FileInfo**. You first need to create an instance of **FileInfo**.

```
String path = @"C:\temp\note.txt";
FileInfo fileInfo = new FileInfo(path);
using (FileStream fileStream = fileInfo.Create())
{
    // do something with fileStream
}
```

There are benefits of choosing **FileInfo** over **File**. For example, you can easily get the file extension by calling the **Extension** property on a **FileInfo**. In addition, you can obtain a **FileInfo**'s parent directory by invoking the **Parent** property. This is not to mention that its **Length** property returns the file size in bytes, **CreationTime** returns the creation time, **isReadOnly** indicates if the file is read-only, and **Exists** returns a boolean that indicates if the file exists.

The last property, **Exists**, probably caught your attention. How can a file not exist if you have created a **FileInfo** that points to the file? The truth is, creating a **FileInfo** simply creates an object in memory and does not create a file. You still need to call **Create** to create the file. Of course, if you pass the path to an existing file when creating a **FileInfo**, its **Exists** property will return true.

The **DirectoryInfo** class is similar to **FileInfo** and offers a similar set of properties, such as **CreationTime**, **Exists**, **Extension**, and **Parent**. **DirectoryInfo** also provides methods for creating and deleting a directory, obtaining the list of subdirectories, and retrieving the list of files in the directory. Here is the signature of **GetFiles**, which returns an array of **FileInfo**s.

```
public FileInfo[] GetFiles()
```

And, here is the signature of **GetDirectories**, which returns an array of **DirectoryInfo**s, each of which represents a subdirectory of the current directory.

```
public FileInfo[] GetDirectories()
```

Listing Files in A Directory

The easiest way to get the file list in a directory is to use the **GetFiles** method of the **Directory** class. Here is code that prints all files in C drive.

```
string[] paths = Directory.GetFiles(@"C:\");
foreach (string path in paths)
{
    Console.WriteLine(path);
}
```

Note that **Directory.GetFiles** returns a string array. Each element of the array contains a full path to the file, e.g. C:\markets.doc.

Alternatively, you can create a **DirectoryInfo** and call its **GetFiles** method, like this:

```
DirectoryInfo directoryInfo = new DirectoryInfo("C:\\");
FileInfo[] files = directoryInfo.GetFiles();
foreach (FileInfo file in files)
{
    Console.WriteLine(file.Name);
}
```

DirectoryInfo.GetFiles returns an array of **FileInfo**s, unlike **Directory.GetFiles** that returns a string array.

Copying and Moving Files

Copying a file is easy. You can create a copy of a file by calling the static method **Copy** on the **File** class. For example, the following single line of code creates a copy of **market.pdf** in C:\temp to **market2.pdf** in C:\temp.

```
File.Copy(@"C:\temp\market.pdf", @"C:\temp\market2.pdf");
```

To move a file, use the **Move** static method in **File**. This code snippet moves **C:\temp\research.pdf** to C:\research.pdf.

```
File.Move(@"C:\temp\research.pdf", @"C:\research.pdf");
```

Input/Output Streams

I/O streams can be likened to water pipes. Just like water pipes connect city houses to a water reservoir, a stream connects C# code to a "data reservoir." This "data reservoir" is called a sink and could be a file, a network socket, or memory. The good thing about streams is you employ a uniform way to transport data from and to different sinks, hence simplifying your code. You just need to construct the correct stream.

All streams derive from the **System.IO.Stream** absract class. You do not work with **Stream** directly, but rather use one of its descendants like **FileStream**, **MemoryStream**, or **NetworkStream**. You've seen **FileStream** in action in the previous section. When you create a file using **File.Create**, for example, a **FileStream** is created for you that allows you to write to the file.

Working with streams directly is hard as you'll have to manage the stream of data yourself. Fortunately, the **System.IO** namespace provides several utility classes to work with a stream. Each utility class falls into one of two groups, it's either a reader or a writer.

The following are the most commonly used readers and writers.

- **StreamReader**. A utility class for reading characters from a stream.

- **StreamWriter**. A utility class for writing characters to a stream.
- **BinaryReader**. A utility class for reading binary data from a stream.
- **BinaryWriter**. A utility class for writing binary data to a stream.

All these reader and writer classes take a **Stream** as an argument to their constructor, so you just need to make sure you pass the correct stream when creating a reader or a writer. For instance, if you want to read a text file, you need to obtain a **FileStream** that points to the file. Most often, a **FileStream** is created for you when you call one of the methods in the **File** class, such as **Create**. In addition, methods in the **File** class may already return a reader or a writer without you having to explicitly create a **FileStream**. For instance, the **File** class's **OpenText** method returns a **StreamReader** that is linked to the underlying file.

The following sections show how to read and write characters and binary data from a file.

Reading Text (Characters)

You use the **StreamReader** class to read characters from a stream. Most of the time, you'll be working with file streams as these are the most popular type of stream. However, there are other kinds of streams too, such as network streams and memory streams.

You can create a **StreamReader** by passing a **Stream** to its constructor:

```
StreamReader streamReader = new StreamReader(stream);
```

However, you may not need to create a **StreamReader** explicitly. The **OpenText** method of the **File** class, for instance, returns a **StreamReader** that is associated with a **FileStream**. Therefore, you can call **OpenText** and obtain a **StreamReader**, like so:

```
StreamReader reader = File.OpenText(path)
```

This is the same as creating a **FileStream** and pass it to the **StreamReader** class's constructor:

```
FileStream fileStream = [create/obtain a FileStream];
```

```
StreamReader streamReader = new StreamReader(fileStream);
```

Regardless of how you create a **StreamReader**, once you have an instance, you can call the various **Read** methods on the **StreamReader**. This **Read** method overload returns the next character in the stream. Here is its signature.

```
public override int Read()
```

Note that it returns the character as an **int**, so to print the character you need to cast it to a char, like this:

```
StreamReader streamReader = ...
char c = (char) streamReader.Read();
```

Reading one character at a time is probably not the most efficient way to go. Often times, you want to read in many characters in one read. For this, you can use this overload of the **Read** method:

```
public override int Read(char[] buffer, int index, int count)
```

This **Read** method overload reads the next *count* characters from the stream and copy them to the char array used as the first argument. The *index* argument (the second argument) indicates the start of char array to write to. If *index* is zero, then the first element of the array will get the first character read. The method returns the number of characters actually read.

Here is an example of reading a block of characters from a stream.

```
StreamReader streamReader = ...
char[] buffer = new char[100];
streamReader.Read(buffer, 0, 100);
// buffer now contains characters read from the stream
```

There is also a **ReadLine** method that reads a line of text from the stream and return it as a string. Its signature is as follows.

```
public override string ReadLine()
```

Listing 14.1 shows code that reads characters from a text file.

Listing 14.1: Reading characters from a file

```
using System;
using System.IO;
```

```
namespace StreamReaderExample
{
    class Program
    {
        static void Main(string[] args)
        {
            String path = "C:\\temp\\today.txt";
            try
            {
                using (StreamReader reader = File.OpenText(path))
                {
                    string line;
                    // Read and display lines from the file
                    while ((line = reader.ReadLine()) != null)
                    {
                        Console.WriteLine(line);
                    }
                }
            }
            catch (IOException e)
            {
                Console.Write(e.Message);
            }

            Console.ReadKey();
        }
    }
}
```

The code in Listing 14.1 opens the **today.txt** file in **C:\temp** and reads and prints each line of text in the file. To test this code, make sure you create a **today.txt** file in the **forementioned** directory.

Writing Text (Characters)

To write text or characters to a stream, use the **StreamWriter** class. This class offers more than a dozen of **Write** methods for various data types, so that there is no need to first convert a non-string to a string. There is one for a **Single**, one for **Uint32**, one for a **char**, and so on. Here are some of the signatures of the **Write** methods:

```
public virtual void Write(bool value)
public virtual void Write(char value)
public virtual void Write(int value)
public virtual void Write(double value)
public virtual void Write(string value)
```

There is also an overload that allows you to write a block of characters in one single operation:

```
public virtual void Write(char[] buffer, int index, int count)
```

In this case, *buffer* contains the characters to write, *index* indicates the start element in the array, and *count* indicates the number of characters in buffer to write.

There are also **WriteLine** methods that accept a value. To the end of the value the method adds a line terminator. Here are the signatures of some of the **WriteLine** method overloads.

```
public virtual void WriteLine()
public virtual void WriteLine(bool value)
public virtual void WriteLine(char value)
public virtual void WriteLine(int value)
public virtual void WriteLine(double value)
public virtual void WriteLine(string value)
```

The first overload that does not take arguments is used to add a line terminator to the stream.

The code in Listing 14.2 receives input from the console and writes it to a file. It keeps on reading until the user enters an empty string.

Listing 14.2: Writing text to a file

```
using System;
using System.IO;

namespace StreamWriterExample
{
    class Program
    {
        static void Main(string[] args)
        {
            Console.WriteLine(
                "Please type in some text. " +
                "Keep typing until you're tired." +
```

```
            "Enter an empty line to exit");
        using (StreamWriter writer =
            new StreamWriter(@"C:\temp\yoursay.txt"))
        {
            String input = Console.ReadLine();
            while (input.Trim().Length != 0)
            {
                writer.WriteLine(input);
                input = Console.ReadLine();
            }
        }
    }
}
}
```

Reading and Writing Binary Data

To read binary data from a file you use the **BinaryReader** class. It's easy to create a **BinaryReader**, you just need to pass a stream to its constructor:

```
BinaryReader reader = new BinaryReader(stream);
```

Then, you call one of its **Read** methods. To read an integer, for example, you call its **ReadInt16** or **ReadInt32** method. To read a double, invoke its **ReadDouble** method. Other methods of **BinaryReader** include **ReadBoolean**, **ReadChar**, **ReadByte**, **ReadDecimal**, **ReadInt64**, and **ReadString**.

To write binary data to a file, use **BinaryWriter**. Like **BinaryReader**, **BinaryWriter** is also very easy to create an instance of. You just pass a stream to its constructor:

```
BinaryWriter writer = new BinaryWriter(stream);
```

BinaryWriter offers a multitude of **Write** method overloads. In fact, there is one **Write** method for each data type, so you can write an integer, a double, a decimal, and so on.

The example in Listing 14.3 shows how you write ten integers to the **numbers.dat** file in C:\temp and read them back.

Listing 14.3: Reading and writing binary data

```csharp
using System;
using System.IO;

namespace BinaryReaderWriterExample
{
    class Program
    {
        static void Main(string[] args)
        {
            string path = @"C:\temp\numbers.dat";
            Random random = new Random();
            FileStream fileStream = File.OpenWrite(path);
            using (BinaryWriter writer =
                    new BinaryWriter(fileStream))
            {
                for (int i = 0; i < 10; i++)
                {
                    writer.Write(random.Next(0, 100));
                }
            }

            fileStream = File.OpenRead(path);
            using (BinaryReader reader =
                    new BinaryReader(fileStream))
            {
                for (int i = 0; i < 10; i++)
                {
                    int number = reader.ReadInt32();
                    Console.WriteLine(number);
                }
            }

            Console.ReadKey();
        }
    }
}
```

If you run the program, you'll see ten numbers between 0 and 100. Each time you run the program, you'll see a different set of numbers as each number is randomly generated using a **Random** object.

Summary

Input/output operations are supported through the members of the **System.IO** namespace. File and directory handling and manipulation are done through the **File**, **Directory**, **FileInfo**, and **DirectoryInfo** classes. Reading and writing data are achieved through streams. In this chapter you learned how to use these classes to read and write characters and binary data from and to a file: **StreamReader**, **StreamWriter**, **BinaryReader**, and **BinaryWriter**.

Chapter 15
Windows Presentation
Foundation

Thus far, all examples in the previous chapters have been built as console applications. There is another type of application that appeals to many people, the desktop application. It's now time to unwrap Windows Presentation Foundation (WPF), the technology that you can use for developing desktop application.

This chapter introduces WPF and builds a couple of simple applications. Note that what is covered in this chapter is only the tip of iceberg of what you can do with WPF. If you're interested to learn more about this technology, you should get a book that specializes in WPF and visit http://windowsclient.net, the official Microsoft WPF and Windows Forms site.

Overview

The .NET Framework version 1.0 shipped with two technologies for developing desktop applications, Windows Forms and GDI+. With the release of .NET 3.0, Microsoft replaced both with Windows Presentation Foundation (WPF). So, why the change of heart? Simple. WPF integrates various technologies that .NET desktop developers had to master if they were to use windows forms and GDI+. WPF is a better solution and you should use it if you're developing a new desktop application.

There are two approaches with regard to developing WPF applications:

- by using code only
- by using code and XAML

I explain both methods in this chapter, first by using code only to build WPF applications and then by employing code and XAML.

Application and Window

This section explains two important classes in developing WPF applications, the **System.Windows.Application** and **System.Windows.Window** classes. It provides two examples at the end of the section.

A WFP application is represented by an instance of the **System.Windows.Application** class or an instance of a class that extends **System.Windows.Application**. After you create an **Application** object, call its **Run** method to start the application. It's that easy.

The **Run** method has two overloads:

```
public int Run()
public int Run(Window window)
```

The second overload takes a **System.Windows.Window** object that represents a window. Without a window, you have nothing visual. The first **Run** overload is normally used when you create a class that extends **Application** and window creation takes place in a method that automatically gets called when you start your application. You will see both **Run** methods used in the projects that accompany this chapter.

An important thing to remember when creating a WPF application is that you must use the **[STAThread]** attribute to annotate your **Main** method. What is this attribute good for? This attribute changes the apartment state of the current thread to be single threaded. WPF applications must be single-threaded. If you forget to apply this attribute, your WPF application will crash.

Now let's first shift our attention to the **Window** class. As the name implies, **Window** represents a window. On it you can add controls such as labels, text boxes, and buttons. Controls are explained in more detail in the section "WPF Controls" later in this chapter.

Property	Description
Content	The content of the **Window**
ContextMenu	The context menu of the **Window**
FontFamily	The font family to be used in the **Window**
FontSize	The font size to be used in the **Window**
FontStyle	The font style to be used in the **Window**
Height	The height of the **Window** in pixels.
Icon	The icon object used by the **Window**
IsActive	Whether or not the **Window** is active
IsVisible	Whether or not the **Window** is visible
Left	The position of the **Window**'s left edge relative to the desktop's left edge.
MaxHeight	The maximum height of the **Window**
MaxWidth	The maximum width of the **Window**
MinHeight	The minimum height of the **Window**
MinWidth	The minimum width of the **WIndow**
Opacity	A double value ranging from 0.0 to 1.0 that determines the **Window**'s opacity, with 1.0 the default value.
Padding	The padding to lay out controls inside the **Window**
Parent	The parent control of the **Window**
Title	The title of the **Window**
Top	The position of the **Window**'s top edge relative to the desktop's top edge.
Width	The width of the **Window**
WindowStartupLocation	The location of the **Window** when it is first started
WindowState	The state the **Window** is in. Its value may be one of the three members of the **WindowState** enumeration (**Minimized, Maximized, Normal**)

Table 15.1: The more important properties of Window

The most important method of **Window** is **Show**. **Show** opens a window and returns without waiting for the newly opened window to be closed. If you don't call **Show**, your pretty window will never show. Here is the signature of **Show**:

```
public void Show()
```

Another member of **Window** you should know by heart is the **Content** property, which is of type **Object**. You can assign any object to this property, but you typically assign a control or a panel. A panel is an area that contains other controls and is discussed in the section "Panels and Layout" later in this chapter.

Table 15.1 lists some of the more important properties in the **Window** class.Now that you know enough theory behind WPF, let's create two simple WPF applications that use **Application**, **Window**, and a control.

Simple WPF Application 1

In this example, you create a WPF application using the **Application** class and starting it by passing a **Window** object.

Listing 15.1: Simple WPF 1

```
using System;
using System.Windows;
using System.Windows.Controls;

namespace App15
{
    class SimpleWPF1
    {
        // WPF apps should execute on a STA thread
        [STAThread]
        static void Main(string[] args)
        {
            Window window = new Window();
            Label label = new Label();
            label.Content = "The WPF is cool";
            window.Content = label;
            window.Title = "Simple WPF App";
            window.Height = 100;
            window.Width = 300;
```

```
        window.WindowStartupLocation =
                WindowStartupLocation.CenterScreen;
        Application app = new Application();
        app.Run(window);
    }
  }
}
```

The code in Listing 15.1 is straight forward enough. First you create a **Window** object and a **Label** object. Then, you give the label a string content and set the label as the window's content. Next, you set the **Title**, **Height**, **Width**, and **WindowStartupLocation** properties of the window and your window is ready. Afterward you instantiate the **Application** class and call its **Run** method.

Now set the **SimpleWPF1** project as the default project in your Visual Studio Express solution and press F5. Voila... you'll see a window just like that in Figure 15.1.

Figure 15.1: Your first simple WPF application

It looks like a standard window complete with Minimize, Restore, and Close buttons. If you press the Close button, the window will close and the application will terminate.

Simple WPF Application 2

Recall that the **Application** class's **Run** method has an overload that takes no argument. You may wonder how you can pass a **Window** to the application if you're using this **Run** overload. The answer is calling any overload of **Run** will cause the **OnStartup** method of the **Application** instance to be called. By writing code that creates a **Window** object here, you can achieve the same goal as passing a **Window** to the other **Run** method. In this example, you create a WPF application by extending the **Application** class and delegate the window creation to its **OnStartup** method.

The code is presented in Listing 15.2.

Listing 15.2: Creating an WPF application by extending Application

```
using System;
using System.Windows;
using System.Windows.Controls;

namespace App15
{
    class SimpleWpf2 : Application
    {
        // WPF apps should execute on a STA thread
        [STAThread]
        static void Main(string[] args)
        {
            SimpleWpf2 app = new SimpleWpf2();
            app.Run();
        }

        protected override void OnStartup(StartupEventArgs e)
        {
            base.OnStartup(e);
            Calendar calendar = new Calendar();
            Window window = new Window();
            window.Title = "WPF 2";
            window.Height = 205;
            window.Width = 200;
            window.Content = calendar;

            window.WindowStartupLocation =
                WindowStartupLocation.CenterScreen;
            window.Show();
        }
    }
}
```

This code is contained in the **SimpleWPF2** project. To run it, set **SimpleWPF2** as the default project and press F5 in your Visual Studio Express solution. You'll see a window that contains a calendar like the one in Figure 15.2.

Figure 15.2: Another simple WPF application

WPF Controls

You've seen two controls used in the previous examples, **Label** and **Calendar**. The .NET Framework provides dozens of ready-to-use controls like **Label** and **Calendar**. The simple ones include **Label**, **TextBox** and **Button**. The more complex ones are controls like **Calendar**, **RichTextBox**, and **WebBrowser**. There are also panels, which are controls that contain other controls. **DockPanel**, **Grid**, and **StackPanel** are examples of panels.

Here is an incomplete list of WPF controls.

- **Border**. Represents a border that can be used to decorate another control.
- **Button**. Represents a clickable button.
- **Calendar**. Represents a scrollable calendar.
- **Canvas**. Represents a blank screen to contain child elements.
- **CheckBox**. Represents a check box.
- **ComboBox**. Represents a combo box with a drop-down list.
- **DataGrid**. Represents a control that displays data in a customizable grid.
- **DatePicker**. Represents a control to select a date from.

- **DockPanel**. Represents a panel where its child elements can be arranged horizontally or vertically, relative to each other.
- **Grid**. Represents a panel with a grid area consisting of rows and columns.
- **Image**. Represents a control to show an image.
- **Label**. Represents a non-editable piece of text.
- **ListBox**. Represents a list of options.
- **Menu**. Represents a menu with elements that can be organized hierarchically.
- **Panel**. Represents a base class for all Panel elements.
- **PasswordBox**. Represents a control for entering passwords.
- **PrintDialog**. Represents a **Print** dialog box.
- **ProgressBar**. Represents a progress bar.
- **RadioButton**. Represents a radio button.
- **RichTextBox**. Represents a rich editing control.
- **Separator**. Represents a control for separating items in items controls.
- **Slider**. Represents a slider control.
- **SpellCheck**. Functions as a spell checker to a text-editing controls such as a **TextBox** or a **RichTextBox**.
- **StackPanel**. A panel that can contain child elements that can be arranged into a single line horizontally or vertically.
- **TabControl**. Represents a control that contains items that occupy the same space on the screen.
- **TextBox**. Represents a control that can display text and let the user edit it.
- **ToolBar**. Represents a container for a group of commands or other controls.
- **ToolTip**. Represents a tooltip.
- **TreeView**. Represents a control that displays data in a tree structure.
- **Validation**. Provides support for data validation.
- **WebBrowser**. Represents a web browser that can be embedded into a WPF application.

You'll see some of these controls used in the examples to come.

Panels and Layout

It is very rare to have a WPF application with only one control. Most of the time, you'll use many controls in your application. In this case, those controls must be arranged into a container such as a panel. A panel is a rectangular shape to which child elements can be added to. The **System.Windows.Controls.Panel** class represents a panel and a couple of implementations are provided in the same namespace. A panel can contain other panels.

When working with a panel, you have to worry about how child controls should be laid out. The code in Listing 15.3 shows how to use a panel and lay out its controls.

Listing 15.3: Panel Example

```
using System;
using System.Windows;
using System.Windows.Controls;

namespace App15
{
    class PanelExample : Application
    {
        // WPF apps should execute on a STA thread
        [STAThread]
        static void Main(string[] args)
        {
            PanelExample app = new PanelExample();
            app.Run();
        }

        protected override void OnStartup(StartupEventArgs e)
        {
            base.OnStartup(e);
            PanelWindow window = new PanelWindow();
            window.Title = "Panel Example";
            window.Height = 228;
            window.Width = 200;

            window.WindowStartupLocation =
                WindowStartupLocation.CenterScreen;
```

```
                window.Show();
            }
    }


class PanelWindow : Window
{
    public PanelWindow()
    {
        StackPanel mainPanel = new StackPanel();
        Calendar calendar = new Calendar();
        Button button1 = new Button();
        button1.Content = "Previous Year";
        Button button2 = new Button();
        button2.Content = "Next Year";

        StackPanel buttonPanel = new StackPanel();
        buttonPanel.Orientation = Orientation.Horizontal;
        buttonPanel.HorizontalAlignment =
            System.Windows.HorizontalAlignment.Center;
        buttonPanel.Children.Add(button1);
        buttonPanel.Children.Add(button2);

        mainPanel.Children.Add(calendar);
        mainPanel.Children.Add(buttonPanel);


        this.Content = mainPanel;
    }
  }
}
```

Figure 15.3: Using Panels

As you can see in Figure 15.3, there are a couple controls that are laid out nicely. The good thing about using the provided layout is that when you resize the window, the layout is retained, as shown in Figure 15.4.

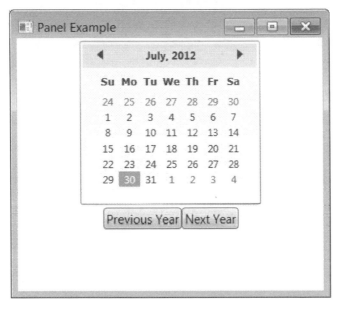

Figure 15.4: Panel Example (enlarged)

The Previous Year and Next Year buttons are meant to allow the user to change year. When you click either of them, however, nothing happens. This is expected because we did not instruct our application how to react. To make something happen when an event takes place (such as when the user clicks on a button), you need to write an event handler. This topic is covered in the next section "Event Handling."

Event Handling

Event handling is a programming paradigm in which a set of instructions are executed upon an event being raised. This is one of the powerful features of WPF as nothing much can be achieved without an event handling capability.

Listing 15.4 presents a class that shows how you can write an event handling method and link it to an event.

Listing 15.4: Event handling

```
using System;
using System.Windows;
using System.Windows.Controls;

namespace App15
{
    class EventExample : Application
    {
        // WPF apps should execute on a STA thread
        [STAThread]
        static void Main(string[] args)
        {
            EventExample app = new EventExample();
            app.Run();
        }

        protected override void OnStartup(StartupEventArgs e)
        {
            base.OnStartup(e);
            EventWindow window = new EventWindow();
            window.Title = "Event Example";
            window.Height = 228;
            window.Width = 200;

            window.WindowStartupLocation =
                WindowStartupLocation.CenterScreen;
            window.Show();
        }
    }

    class EventWindow : Window
    {
        Calendar calendar;
        public EventWindow()
        {
            StackPanel mainPanel = new StackPanel();
            calendar = new Calendar();
            Button button1 = new Button();
            button1.Content = "Highlight";
            Button button2 = new Button();
            button2.Content = "No Highlight";
```

```
        StackPanel buttonPanel = new StackPanel();
        buttonPanel.Orientation = Orientation.Horizontal;
        buttonPanel.HorizontalAlignment =
            System.Windows.HorizontalAlignment.Center;
        buttonPanel.Children.Add(button1);
        buttonPanel.Children.Add(button2);

        mainPanel.Children.Add(calendar);
        mainPanel.Children.Add(buttonPanel);

        button1.Click += OnClick1;
        button2.Click += OnClick2;

        this.Content = mainPanel;
    }

    void OnClick1(object sender, RoutedEventArgs e)
    {
        calendar.IsTodayHighlighted = true;
    }
    void OnClick2(object sender, RoutedEventArgs e)
    {
        calendar.IsTodayHighlighted = false;
    }
  }
}
```

Pay special attention to the lines in bold.

```
        button1.Click += OnClick1;
        button2.Click += OnClick2;
```

These lines basically inform WPF that the **Click** event of **button1** is linked to **OnClick1** and the **Click** event of **button2** to **OnClick2**. **OnClick1** and **OnClick2** are event handlers and change the value of the **IsTodayHighlighted** property of the **Calendar** control.

```
    void OnClick1(object sender, RoutedEventArgs e)
    {
        calendar.IsTodayHighlighted = true;
    }
    void OnClick2(object sender, RoutedEventArgs e)
    {
        calendar.IsTodayHighlighted = false;
```

```
    }
```

Running the code in Listing 15.4 shows a window with a calendar with two buttons like that in Figure 15.5. The buttons are now 'live' as they are connected to event handlers.

Figure 15.5: A WPF application with event handlers

XAML

XAML stands for eXtensible Application Markup Language. Originally created for use with WPF, XAML can be used for any hierarchical data type.

When you create a WPF project using Visual Studio Express, two .xaml files will be created for you. The first file, **MainWindow.xaml**, describes the main window in your WPF application. It looks like this.

```
<Window x:Class="XamlExample1.MainWindow"
   xmlns="http://schemas.microsoft.com/winfx/2006/xaml/presentation"
   xmlns:x="http://schemas.microsoft.com/winfx/2006/xaml"
   Title="MainWindow" Height="350" Width="525">

   <Grid>

   </Grid>
```

```
</Window>
```

By default, it uses a **Grid** as the primary panel for all your controls. However, you can easily change this.

The second XAML file created for you when you start a WPF project is an **App.xaml** file. It looks like this:

```
<Application x:Class="XamlExample1.App"
   xmlns="http://schemas.microsoft.com/winfx/2006/xaml/presentation"
   xmlns:x="http://schemas.microsoft.com/winfx/2006/xaml"
   StartupUri="MainWindow.xaml">

   <Application.Resources>

   </Application.Resources>
</Application>
```

This file describes the WPF application. Be aware that the **Application** element contains a **StartupUri** attribute that references the **MainWindow.xaml** file that defines the **Window** object.

If you run the project, you'll see a blank window.

The following example features a XAML-based WPF application. Listing 15.5 shows its **MainWindow.xaml** file and Listing 15.6 its **App.xaml** file.

Listing 15.5: The MainWindow.xaml file

```
<Window x:Class="XamlExample2.MainWindow"

      xmlns="http://schemas.microsoft.com/winfx/2006/xaml/presentat
      ion"
      xmlns:x="http://schemas.microsoft.com/winfx/2006/xaml"
      Title="MainWindow" Height="350" Width="525">
   <DockPanel LastChildFill="True">
     <Label Foreground="Green" Background="Bisque"
     DockPanel.Dock="Top"
           Height="100"
     HorizontalContentAlignment="Center">Top</Label>
     <Label Foreground="Red" Background="Beige"
     DockPanel.Dock="Left"
```

```
                    Width="50"
        VerticalContentAlignment="Center">Left</Label>
          <TextBlock Foreground="Blue" Background="AliceBlue"
                    DockPanel.Dock="Right">Right</TextBlock>
    </DockPanel>
</Window>
```

Listing 15.6: The App.xaml file

```
<Application x:Class="XamlExample2.App"
   xmlns="http://schemas.microsoft.com/winfx/2006/xaml/presentation"
   xmlns:x="http://schemas.microsoft.com/winfx/2006/xaml"
   StartupUri="MainWindow.xaml">

   <Application.Resources>

   </Application.Resources>
</Application>
```

As you can see from the XAML example, the application does not contains a single line of code. All you had to do so far was configure the application. If it were to be written without XAML, the application would look like the code in Listing 15.7.

Listing 15.7: Code Only Equivalent of the XAML example

```
using System;
using System.Windows;
using System.Windows.Controls;
using System.Windows.Media;

namespace XamlExample2
{
    class CodeOnly : Application
    {
        // WPF apps should execute on a STA thread
        [STAThread]
        static void Main(string[] args)
        {
            CodeOnly app = new CodeOnly();
            app.Run();
        }

        protected override void OnStartup(StartupEventArgs e)
        {
            base.OnStartup(e);
            Window window = new Window();
```

```
window.Title = "CodeOnly Equivalent";
window.Height = 350;
window.Width = 525;

DockPanel dockPanel = new DockPanel();
dockPanel.LastChildFill = true;

Label topElement = new Label();
topElement.Content = "Top";
DockPanel.SetDock(topElement, Dock.Top);
topElement.Foreground =
    new SolidColorBrush(Colors.Green);
topElement.Background =
    new SolidColorBrush(Colors.Bisque);
topElement.Height = 100;
topElement.HorizontalContentAlignment =
    HorizontalAlignment.Center;

Label leftElement = new Label();
leftElement.Content = "Left";
leftElement.Foreground =
    new SolidColorBrush(Colors.Red);
leftElement.Background =
    new SolidColorBrush(Colors.Beige);
leftElement.Width = 50;
leftElement.VerticalContentAlignment =
    VerticalAlignment.Center;
DockPanel.SetDock(leftElement, Dock.Left);

TextBox rightElement = new TextBox();
rightElement.Text = "Right";
rightElement.Foreground =
    new SolidColorBrush(Colors.Blue);
rightElement.Background =
    new SolidColorBrush(Colors.AliceBlue);
DockPanel.SetDock(rightElement, Dock.Right);

dockPanel.Children.Add(topElement);
dockPanel.Children.Add(leftElement);
dockPanel.Children.Add(rightElement);

window.Content = dockPanel;
window.Show();
}
}
```

```
}
```

Summary

WPF is the latest .NET technology for developing desktop applications. In this chapter you have learned the two main classes in WPF, **Application** and **Window**, as well as used several controls. You've also learned that you can write WPF applications by writing code or by using XAML and code.

Chapter 16
Polymorphism

Polymorphism is the hardest concept to explain to those new to object-oriented programming (OOP). In fact, most of the time its definition would not make sense without an example or two. Well, try this. Here is the definition in many programming books: "Polymorphism is an OOP feature that enables an object to determine which method implementation to invoke upon receiving a method call." If you find this hard to digest, you're not alone. Polymorphism is hard to explain in simple language, even though it is easy enough to understand if accompanied by an example or two.

This chapter starts with a simple example that should make polymorphism crystal clear. It then proceeds with another example that demonstrates the use of polymorphism in a simple Draw application.

Note
In other programming languages, polymorphism is also called late-binding or runtime-binding or dynamic binding.

Defining Polymorphism

In C# and other OOP languages, it is legal to assign to a reference variable an object whose type is different from the variable type, if certain conditions are met. In essence, if you have a reference variable **a** whose type is **A**, it is legal to assign an object of type **B**, like this

```
A a = new B();
```

provided one of the following conditions is met.

- **A** is a class and **B** is a subclass of **A**.
- **A** is an interface and **B** or one of its parents implements **A**.

As you have learned in Chapter 6, "Inheritance," this is called upcasting.

When you assign **a** an instance of **B** like in the preceding code, **a** is of type **A**. This means, you cannot call a method in **B** that is not defined in A. However, if you print the value of **a.GetType().ToString()**, you'll get "B" and not "A." So, what does this mean? At compile time, the type of **a** is **A**, so the compiler will not allow you to call a method in **B** that is not defined in **A**. On the other hand, at runtime the type of **a** is **B**, as proven by the return value of **a.GetType().ToString()**.

Now, here comes the essence of polymorphism. If **B** overrides a method (say, a method named **Play**) in **A**, calling **a.Play()** will cause the implementation of **Play** in **B** (and not in **A**) to be invoked. Polymorphism enables an object (in this example, the one referenced by **a**) to determine which method implementation to choose (either the one in **A** or the one in **B**) when a method is called. Polymorphism dictates that the implementation in the runtime object be invoked.

What if you call another method in **a** (say, a method called **Stop**) and the method is not implemented in **B**? The CLR will be smart enough to know this and look into the inheritance hierarchy of **B**. **B**, as it happens, must be a subclass of **A** or, if **A** is an interface, a subclass of another class that implements **A**. Otherwise, the code would not have compiled. Having figured this out, the CLR will climb the ladder of the class hierarchy and find the implementation of **Stop** and execute it.

Now, there is more sense in the definition of polymorphism: Polymorphism is an OOP feature that enables an object to determine which method implementation to invoke upon receiving a method call.

Technically, though, how does C# achieve this? The C# compiler, as it turns out, upon encountering a method call such as **a.Play()**, checks if the class/interface represented by **a** defines such a method (a **Play** method) and if the correct set of parameters are passed to the method. But, that is the farthest the compiler goes. With the exception of static and sealed methods, it does not connect (or bind) a method call with a method body. The CLR determines how to bind a method call with the method body at runtime. In other words, except for static and sealed methods, method binding in C# takes place at runtime and not at compile time. Runtime binding is also called late binding or dynamic binding. The opposite is early binding, in which binding occurs at compile time or link time. Early binding happens in languages like C.

Therefore, polymorphism is made possible by the late binding mechanism in the .NET Framework. Because of this, polymorphism is rather inaccurately also called late-binding or dynamic binding or runtime binding.

Let's look at the code in Listing 16.1.

Listing 16.1: An example of polymorphism

```csharp
using System;

namespace PolymorphismExample1
{
    class Employee {
        public virtual void Work()
        {
            Console.WriteLine("I am an employee.");
        }
    }

    class Manager : Employee
    {
        public override void Work()
        {
            Console.WriteLine("I am a manager.");
        }

        public void Manage()
        {
            Console.WriteLine("Managing ...");
        }
    }

    class Program
    {
```

```
static void Main(string[] args)
{
    Employee employee;
    employee = new Manager();
    Console.WriteLine(employee.GetType().ToString());
    employee.Work();
    Manager manager = (Manager) employee;
    manager.Manage();

    Console.ReadKey();
}
}
}
```

Listing 16.1 defines two classes: **Employee** and **Manager**. **Employee** has a virtual method called **Work**, and **Manager** extends **Employee** and adds a new method called **Manage** as well as override **Work**.

The **Main** method in the **Program** class defines an object variable called **employee** of type **Employee**:

```
Employee employee;
```

However, **employee** is assigned an instance of **Manager**, as in:

```
employee = new Manager();
```

This is legal because **Manager** is a subclass of **Employee**, so a **Manager** "is an" **Employee**. Because **employee** is assigned an instance of **Manager**, what is the outcome of **employee.GetType().ToString()**? You're right. It's "Manager," not "Employee."

Then, the **work** method is called.

```
employee.Work();
```

Guess what is written on the console?

```
I am a manager.
```

This means that it is the **Work** method in the **Manager** class that got called, which was polymorphism in action.

Now, because the runtime type of **a** is **Manager**, you can downcast **a** to **Manager**, as the code shows:

```
Manager manager = (Manager) employee;
```

```
manager.Manage();
```

After seeing the code, you might ask, why would you declare **employee** as **Employee** in the first place? Why not declare **employee** as type **Manager**, like this?

```
Manager employee;
employee = new Manager();
```

You do this to ensure flexibility in cases where you don't know whether the object reference (**employee**) will be assigned an instance of **Manager** or something else. This technique will become clear as we look at the following examples.

Polymorphism in Action

Suppose you have a WPF application and you have a method named **MakeMoreTransparent** that changes the opacity of a **UIElement**. You want to be able to pass to the method any WPF controls and panels. Because of this, you need to make the method accept a **UIElement**, which is the base class for all UI elements in WPF. Listing 16.2 shows the method.

Listing 16.2: The MakeMoreTransparent method

```
void MakeMoreTransparent(UIElement uiElement)
{
    double opacity = uiElement.Opacity;
    if (opacity > 0.2)
    {
        uiElement.Opacity = opacity - 0.1;
    }
}
```

Thanks to polymorphism, **MakeMoreTransparent** will accept an instance of **UIElement** or an instance of a subclass of **UIElement**. Listing 16.3 shows the complete WPF application, which is a window with a calendar and three buttons. Clicking the third button will iterate over all children of the window and pass each child to **MakeMoreTransparent**.

Listing 16.3: A WPF application with polymorphism

```csharp
using System;
using System.Windows;
using System.Windows.Controls;

namespace PolymorphismExample2
{
    class PolymorphismExample2 : Application
    {
        // WPF apps should execute on a STA thread
        [STAThread]
        static void Main(string[] args)
        {
            PolymorphismExample2 app = new PolymorphismExample2();
            app.Run();
        }

        protected override void OnStartup(StartupEventArgs e)
        {
            base.OnStartup(e);
            EventWindow window = new EventWindow();
            window.Title = "Polymorphism Example";
            window.Height = 228;
            window.Width = 300;

            window.WindowStartupLocation =
                WindowStartupLocation.CenterScreen;
            window.Show();
        }
    }

    class EventWindow : Window
    {
        Calendar calendar;
        public EventWindow()
        {
            StackPanel mainPanel = new StackPanel();
            calendar = new Calendar();
            Button button1 = new Button();
            button1.Content = "Highlight";
            Button button2 = new Button();
            button2.Content = "No Highlight";
            Button button3 = new Button();
            button3.Content = "Make more transparent";
```

```
    StackPanel buttonPanel = new StackPanel();
    buttonPanel.Orientation = Orientation.Horizontal;
    buttonPanel.HorizontalAlignment =
        System.Windows.HorizontalAlignment.Center;
    buttonPanel.Children.Add(button1);
    buttonPanel.Children.Add(button2);
    buttonPanel.Children.Add(button3);

    mainPanel.Children.Add(calendar);
    mainPanel.Children.Add(buttonPanel);



    button1.Click += OnClick1;
    button2.Click += OnClick2;
    button3.Click += OnClick3;


    this.Content = mainPanel;
}

void OnClick1(object sender, RoutedEventArgs e)
{
    calendar.IsTodayHighlighted = true;
}
void OnClick2(object sender, RoutedEventArgs e)
{
    calendar.IsTodayHighlighted = false;
}
void OnClick3(object sender, RoutedEventArgs e)
{
    Panel panel = (Panel) this.Content;
    int childrenCount = panel.Children.Count;
    Console.WriteLine("start");
    foreach (UIElement child in panel.Children)
    {
        MakeMoreTransparent(child);
    }
}



void MakeMoreTransparent(UIElement uiElement)
{
    double opacity = uiElement.Opacity;
    if (opacity > 0.2)
```

```
        {
            uiElement.Opacity = opacity - 0.1;
        }

    }
  }
}
```

If you run the WPF application, you'll see something like the window in Figure 16.1. Click the button on the right repeatedly to see polymorphism in action.

Figure 16.1: WPF with polymorphism

Polymorphism in a Drawing Application

The strength of polymorphism is apparent in situations whereby the programmer does not know in advance the type of object that will be created. For example, consider the Simple Draw application in Figure 16.2. With this application you can draw three types of shapes: rectangles, lines, and ovals.

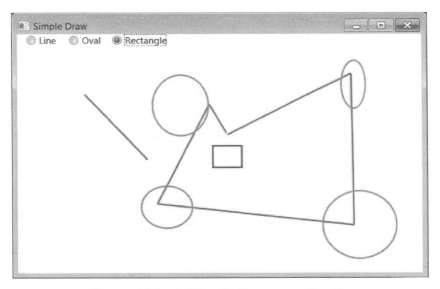

Figure 16.2: A Simple Draw application

To draw a line, for example, first click the Line radio, and then click and drag on the drawing area, and release the mouse button. The position you first click on the drawing area will become the start point (x1, y1). The coordinate on which you release your mouse button will be the end point (x2, y2).

Now let's figure out how the application works.

First, look at the **IShape** interface and its implementation classes (**SimpleLine, SimpleOval,** and **SimpleRectangle**) in Listing 16.4.

Listing 16.4: The IShape interface and its implementations

```
interface IShape
{
    void Draw(Grid myGrid
}

public class SimpleLine : IShape
{
    double x1, y1, x2, y2;
    public SimpleLine(double x1, double y1, double x2, double y2)
    {
        this.x1 = x1;
```

```
            this.y1 = y1;
            this.x2 = x2;
            this.y2 = y2;
        }

    public void Draw(Grid grid)
    {
        // body omitted to save space
    }
}

public class SimpleOval : IShape
{
    double x1, y1, x2, y2;
    public SimpleOval(double x1, double y1, double x2, double y2)
    {
        this.x1 = x1;
        this.y1 = y1;
        this.x2 = x2;
        this.y2 = y2;
    }

    public void Draw(Grid grid)
    {
        // body omitted to save space
    }
}

public class SimpleRectangle : IShape
{
    double x1, y1, x2, y2;

    public SimpleRectangle(double x1, double y1, double x2,
            double y2)
    {
        this.x1 = x1;
        this.y1 = y1;
        this.x2 = x2;
        this.y2 = y2;
    }

    public void Draw(Grid grid)
    {
        // body omitted to save space
    }
}
```

There is only one method in the **IShape** interface, **Draw**. It is meant to be overridden by implementation classes to draw the appropriate shape. In the **SimpleRectangle** class, for example, the **Draw** method has been overridden to draw the shape of a rectangle.

Now, let's examine the complete application. The XAML file is given in Listing 16.5 and the code in Listing 16.6.

Listing 16.5: The MainWindow.xaml file

```
<Window x:Class="SimpleDraw.MainWindow"
  xmlns="http://schemas.microsoft.com/winfx/2006/xaml/presentation"
  xmlns:x="http://schemas.microsoft.com/winfx/2006/xaml"
  Name="idwin"  Title="Simple Draw" Height="350" Width="525"
  MouseDown="canvas1_MouseDown" MouseUp="canvas1_MouseUp">

    <Grid Name="buttonGrid">
        <RadioButton Content="Line" Height="16"
            HorizontalAlignment="Left" Margin="12,0,0,0"
            Name="radioButton1" VerticalAlignment="Top"
            IsChecked="True" Checked="radioButton1_Checked" />
        <RadioButton Content="Oval" Height="16"
            HorizontalAlignment="Left" Margin="66,0,0,0"
            Name="radioButton2" VerticalAlignment="Top"
            Checked="radioButton2_Checked" />
        <RadioButton Content="Rectangle" Height="16"
            HorizontalAlignment="Left" Margin="120,0,0,0"
            Name="radioButton3" VerticalAlignment="Top"
            Checked="radioButton3_Checked" />
    </Grid>
</Window>
```

Listing 16.6: The SimpleDraw application

```
using System;
using System.Windows;
using System.Windows.Controls;
using System.Windows.Input;
using System.Windows.Shapes;

namespace SimpleDraw
{
    /// <summary>
    /// Interaction logic for MainWindow.xaml
    /// </summary>
```

```csharp
public partial class MainWindow : Window
{
    private enum ShapeType
    {
        Line, Oval, Rectangle
    }
    private Point startPoint;
    private Point endPoint;
    private ShapeType shapeType = ShapeType.Line;

    public MainWindow()
    {
        InitializeComponent();
    }


    private void canvas1_MouseDown(object sender,
            MouseButtonEventArgs e)
    {
        startPoint = e.GetPosition(this);
    }

    private void canvas1_MouseUp(object sender,
            MouseButtonEventArgs e)
    {
        endPoint = e.GetPosition(this);
        IShape shape = null;
        if (shapeType == ShapeType.Line)
        {
            shape = new SimpleLine(startPoint.X, startPoint.Y,
                    endPoint.X, endPoint.Y);
        }
        else if (shapeType == ShapeType.Oval)
        {
            shape = new SimpleOval(startPoint.X, startPoint.Y,
                    endPoint.X, endPoint.Y);
        }
        else if (shapeType == ShapeType.Rectangle)
        {
            shape = new SimpleRectangle(startPoint.X,
                    startPoint.Y, endPoint.X, endPoint.Y);
        }

        if (shape != null)
        {
            Grid grid = (Grid) this.FindName("buttonGrid");
```

```
            shape.Draw(grid);
        }
    }

    private void radioButton1_Checked(object sender,
            RoutedEventArgs e)
    {
        shapeType = ShapeType.Line;
    }

    private void radioButton2_Checked(object sender,
            RoutedEventArgs e)
    {
        shapeType = ShapeType.Oval;
    }

    private void radioButton3_Checked(object sender,
            RoutedEventArgs e)
    {
        shapeType = ShapeType.Rectangle;
    }
}


interface IShape
{
    void Draw(Grid myGrid);
}

public class SimpleLine : IShape
{
    double x1, y1, x2, y2;

    public SimpleLine(double x1, double y1, double x2,
            double y2)
    {
        this.x1 = x1;
        this.y1 = y1;
        this.x2 = x2;
        this.y2 = y2;
    }

    public void Draw(Grid grid)
    {
        Line windowLine = new Line();
```

```
            windowLine.X1 = x1;
            windowLine.Y1 = y1;
            windowLine.X2 = x2;
            windowLine.Y2 = y2;
            windowLine.Stroke =
                    System.Windows.Media.Brushes.Magenta;
            windowLine.StrokeThickness = 2;
            grid.Children.Add(windowLine);
        }
    }

    public class SimpleOval : IShape
    {
        double x1, y1, x2, y2;

        public SimpleOval(double x1, double y1, double x2,
                double y2)
        {
            this.x1 = x1;
            this.y1 = y1;
            this.x2 = x2;
            this.y2 = y2;
        }

        public void Draw(Grid grid)
        {
            double x, y;
            Ellipse oval = new Ellipse();
            Thickness margin;
            if (x1 < x2)
            {
                x = x1;
            }
            else
            {
                x = x2;
            }
            if (y1 < y2)
            {
                y = y1;
            }
            else
            {
                y = y2;
            }
            margin = new Thickness(x, y, 0, 0);
```

```
        oval.Margin = margin;
        oval.HorizontalAlignment = HorizontalAlignment.Left;
        oval.VerticalAlignment = VerticalAlignment.Top;
        oval.Stroke = System.Windows.Media.Brushes.LimeGreen;
        oval.Width = Math.Abs(x2 - x1);
        oval.Height = Math.Abs(y2 - y1);
        Canvas.SetLeft(oval, x);
        Canvas.SetTop(oval, y);
        oval.StrokeThickness = 2;
        grid.Children.Add(oval);
    }
}

public class SimpleRectangle : IShape
{
    double x1, y1, x2, y2;

    public SimpleRectangle(double x1, double y1, double x2,
            double y2)
    {
        this.x1 = x1;
        this.y1 = y1;
        this.x2 = x2;
        this.y2 = y2;
    }

    public void Draw(Grid grid)
    {
        double x, y;
        Rectangle rect = new Rectangle();
        if (x1 < x2)
        {
            x = x1;
        }
        else
        {
            x = x2;
        }
        if (y1 < y2)
        {
            y = y1;
        }
        else
        {
            y = y2;
```

```
        }
        Thickness margin = new Thickness(x, y, 0, 0);
        rect.Margin = margin;
        rect.HorizontalAlignment = HorizontalAlignment.Left;
        rect.VerticalAlignment = VerticalAlignment.Top;
        rect.Stroke = System.Windows.Media.Brushes.Red;
        rect.Width = Math.Abs(x2 - x1);
        rect.Height = Math.Abs(y2 - y1);
        Canvas.SetLeft(rect, x);
        Canvas.SetTop(rect, y);
        rect.StrokeThickness = 2;
        grid.Children.Add(rect);
    }
  }
}
```

The **MainWindow** class, a subclass of **System.Windows.Window**, employs a **Grid** that contains three **RadioButton** controls for the user to select a shape to draw. **MainWindow** also has several class variables. The first are two **System.Windows.Point**s, **startPoint** and **endPoint**. **startPoint** indicates the mouse press coordinate on the drawing area. **endPoint** denotes the mouse release coordinate. Then, there is **shapeType**, a reference to **ShapeType**, an enum with three members (**Line**, **Oval**, and **Rectangle**). **shapeType** indicates the selected shape chosen by the user. Its value changes every time the user clicks a different radio button.

Pay special attention to the **canvas1_mouseUp** event handler:

```
private void canvas1_MouseUp(object sender,
        MouseButtonEventArgs e)
{
    endPoint = e.GetPosition(this);
    IShape shape = null;
    if (shapeType == ShapeType.Line)
    {
        shape = new SimpleLine(startPoint.X, startPoint.Y,
                endPoint.X, endPoint.Y);
    }
    else if (shapeType == ShapeType.Oval)
    {
        shape = new SimpleOval(startPoint.X, startPoint.Y,
                endPoint.X, endPoint.Y);
    }
    else if (shapeType == ShapeType.Rectangle)
    {
```

```
        shape = new SimpleRectangle(startPoint.X,
                startPoint.Y, endPoint.X, endPoint.Y);
    }

    if (shape != null)
    {
        Grid grid = (Grid) this.FindName("buttonGrid");
        shape.Draw(grid);
    }
}
```

This is where polymorphism is taking place. First, the event handler obtains the end point, the point on which the user released the mouse. Then, it declares a **shape** variable of type **IShape**. The object assigned to **shape** depends on the value of **shapeType**. In this case, you see that what object to create was not known at the time the class was written. Nor was it known at compile-time.

Finally, the event handler calls the **Draw** method on **shape** to give the object a chance to draw itself on the grid.

Summary

Polymorphism is one of the main pillars in object-oriented programming. It is useful in circumstances where the type of an object is not known at compile time. This chapter demonstrated polymorphism through several examples.

Chapter 17
ADO.NET

ADO.NET is a .NET technology for accessing and manipulating data in various formats, including data stored in a relational database or as XML. The name ADO.NET comes from ADO (Access Data Objects), an old Microsoft technology that offered similar functionality. Despite the name similarity, however, the architecture of ADO.NET bears little resemblance to its predecessor.

Having existed since .NET 1.0, ADO.NET is readily available to developers of any .NET language, including C# programmers. With regard to accessing relational databases, the beauty of ADO.NET is that it offers a uniform way of accessing different relational databases. Different database servers use different proprietary protocols and accessing them without ADO.NET (or a similar technology such as Java Database Connectivity) may require writing entirely different codes. For each relational database supported by ADO.NET, there is a set of classes able to communicate with the database server. This set of classes is called a data provider.

This chapter discusses the basic features of ADO.NET, especially those for accessing and manipulating data in a relational database. It's assumed you have basic knowledge of SQL.

Introduction to ADO.NET

ADO.NET consists of a number of types in the **System.Data** and **System.Data.Common** namespaces, all of which are to be found in the **System.Data.dll** assembly. The tree abstract classes in Table 17.1 are members of **System.Data.Common** and the most important ADO.NET types.

Class	Description
DbConnection	Represents a connection to a database
DbCommand	Represents an SQL statement or stored procedure
DbDataReader	Represents a data reader that can read a forward-only stream of rows/records.

Table 17.1: The most important ADO.NET types

Each of the abstract classes in Table 17.1 implements an interface in **System.Data**. **DbConnection** implements **System.Data.IDbConnection**, **DbCommand** implements **System.Data.IDbCommand**, and **DbDataReader** implements **System.Data.IDbDataReader**.

Since the three types in Table 17.1 are abstract classes, there must be implementations in order for the types to be of practical use. The implementations come in the form of data providers. As it turns out, each DBMS requires a different data provider. That is, an SQL Server database requires a different data provider than that for accessing a Sybase database. However, because all data providers implement the very same core ADO.NET types, you are awarded a uniform way of accessing *different* databases. In other words, you can access and manipulate data in a SQL Server database the same way you would an Oracle database.

Every database needs a different data provider. The .NET class library comes with a data provider for SQL Server, a data provider for Oracle, and data providers for accessing databases indirectly through old technologies OLE DB and ODBC. Today, however, there is at least one data provider for each type of database server on the market. Because .NET is so popular, any database manufacturer has interest in making available a data provider for their product. However, data providers can also come from a third party who does not make a database server. It is not uncommon for popular databases to have various data providers. Databases with no matching data provider can often be used through OLE DB or ODBC. For example, there is no data provider for Microsoft Access databases, but you can access them through OLE DB.

Table 17.2 shows the data providers that come with the .NET Framework. In addition to those in Table 17.2, there is also a data provider for Entity Data Model (EDM) applications, but it is beyond the scope of this book and is therefore not included in the table.

Data Provider	Description
Data provider for SQL Server	For Microsoft SQL Server 7.0 or later, in the **System.Data.SqlClient** namespace.
Data provider for OLE DB	For OLE DB, in the **System.Data.OleDb** namespace
Data provider for ODBC	For ODBC, in the **System.Data.Odbc** namespace.
Data provider for Oracle	For Oracle, in the **System.Data.OracleClient** namespace. Use the data provider from Oracle instead.

Table 17.2: The data providers included in the .NET Framework

Note that accessing a database via OLE DB or ODBC is indirect access that is typically slower than using a data provider. Therefore, you should always try to find a data provider for your selected database first before resorting to OLE DB or ODBC. The following web page provides a list of data providers not supplied by Microsoft:

http://msdn.microsoft.com/en-us/data/dd363565.aspx

Note that to access Oracle databases you should use the data provider from Oracle rather than the one that comes in the .NET class library.

Five Steps to Data Access

Database access and data manipulation through ADO.NET require five steps.

1. Installing the data provider software for the database you want to access, unless the data provider has been included in .NET class library.
2. Obtaining a database connection.
3. Creating a command object that represents an SQL statement.
4. Optionally creating a data reader to read data from the database.

5. Closing ADO.NET objects to free resources. Thanks to the **using** statement, you don't have to do this manually.

These steps are detailed in the following subsections.

Installing the Data Provider

A data provider is a set of classes deployed by a third party. If you're using Microsoft SQL server 7 or later or accessing the database through OLE DB or ODBC, then you can skip this step. If you're using a database other than SQL Server and not using OLE DB or ODBC, you will have to download and install a data provider before you can start accessing the database from your C# code. For example, if you are connecting to a MySQL database, you should download the ADO.NET driver for MySQL (that's the name for the data provider) at http://www.mysql.com/products/connector. A data provider may come as an MSI installer or a ZIP file.

Figure 17.1 shows the installation wizard for MySQL data provider.

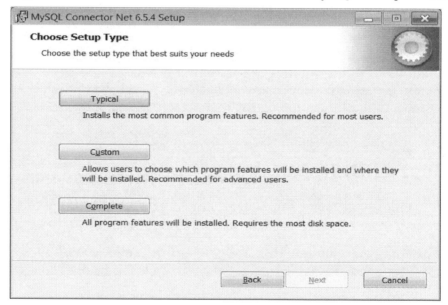

Figure 17.1: Installing ADO.NET data provider for MySQL

After you install the data provider, you should be able to add references to it from within Visual Studio 2010 Express or other IDEs. To add a reference, right-click on the project icon and select **Add Reference**. On the window that shows up, click the .NET tab and scroll to select the assemblies from the window. Figure 17.2 shows the three assemblies for MySQL.

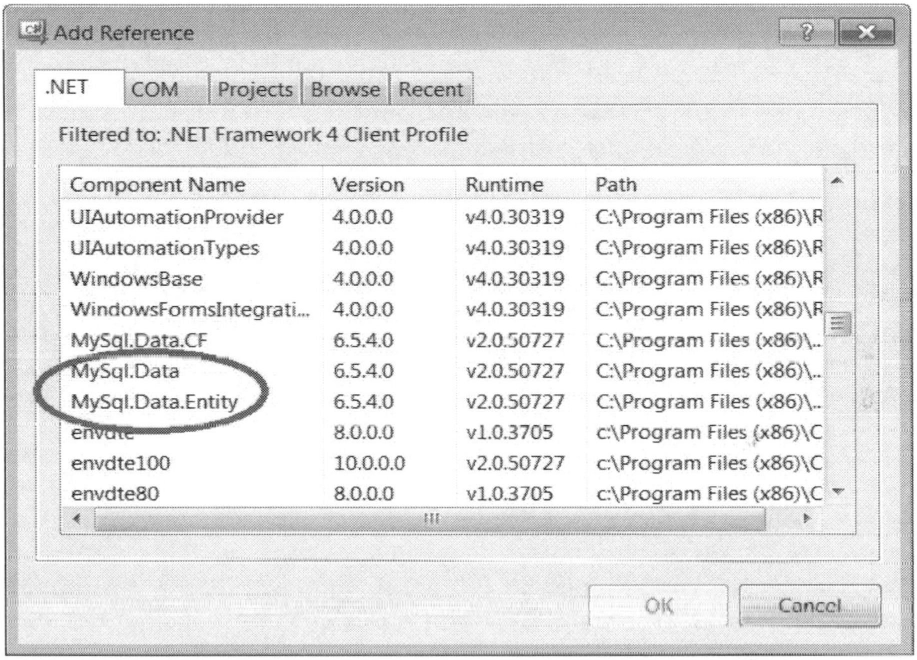

Figure 17.2: Referencing MySQL data provider

Do not select MySql.Data.CF because it contains similar classes as MySql.Data and selecting both will create conflicts. Only use MySql.Data.CF if you're using the .NET Compact Framework (not discussed in this book).

Obtaining a Database Connection

A database connection facilitates communication between your code and a relational database. The **System.Data.Common.DbConnection** abstract class is the template for connection objects. You typically call the constructor of an implementation class and pass a connection string. You need to know the implementation class in the data provider. The name of the class is data provider-specific. For example, in the SQL Server data provider, the class that extends **DbConnection** is **System.Data.SqlClient.SqlConnection**. Thus, to create a connection object for accessing SQL Server, you would write this.

```
SqlConnection connection = new SqlConnection(connectionString);
```

In the MySQL data provider, on other the other hand, a connection is represented by the **MySql.Data.MySqlClient.MySqlConnection** class. Therefore, to create a connection object, you use this code.

```
MySqlConnection connection = new MySqlConnection(connectionString);
```

Since the implementation class is derived from **DbConnection**, it is possible to assign a connection object to a **DbConnection** reference variable, like so

```
DbConnection connection = new SqlConnection(connectionString);
```

or

```
DbConnection connection = new MySqlConnection(connectionString);
```

However, this strategy may not work when constructing a **DbCommand** object because the constructor of the implementation for **DbCommand** requires a specific type of **DbConnection**. For example, this one won't compile if **connection** is of type **DbConnection** because the second argument for the **SqlCommand** class's constructor must be of type **SqlConnection**:

```
SqlCommand command = new SqlCommand(sql, connection);
```

Therefore, you should always assign a connection object to a specific type variable:

```
SqlConnection connection = new SqlConnection(connectionString);
MySqlConnection connection = new MySqlConnection(connectionString);
```

The tricky part is to build the correct connection string. Typically, you need to know the type of the database you're trying to access, the location (host or IP address) of the server, and, optionally, a user name and password for the database. And then, you have to build a string that consists of key/value pairs like these:

```
key-1=value-1; key-2=value-2; ...; key-n=value-n
```

Each key/value pair is separated by a semicolon and the space after a semicolon is optional.

You may also use your Windows credentials to access a database if it supports integrated security.

OK. Let's talk about SQL Server first, since this is most probably your first choice of DBMS.

The keys for the SQL Server connection string can be found here.

http://msdn.microsoft.com/en-us/library/system.data.sqlclient. sqlconnection.connectionstring

Table 17.3 shows some of the more important ones.

Opening a database connection is one of most resource-intensive operations in database manipulation. As such, ADO.NET supports connection pooling, which means that open connections are not closed but simply returned to a pool. The Pooling key in a connection string should be left in its default value unless you have a very good reason not to use connection pooling.

The following example is a connection string to open a connection to a SQL Server database by attaching its MDF file. It also uses the current Windows credentials to authenticate the user.

```
Data Source=.\\SQLEXPRESS;AttachDbFilename=C:\\MarketingDB.mdf;
"Integrated Security=True;Connect Timeout=30
```

The following connection string connects to a SQL Server named PC\\SQLEXPRESS and uses the MyCustomerDB database.

```
Persist Security Info=False;Integrated Security=true;
Initial Catalog=MyCustomerDB;Server=PC\\SQLEXPRESS";
```

Key	Description
AttachedDBFilename or Extended Properties or Initial File Name	The name of the database .mdf file. Other file types are not supported.
Connect Timeout or Connection Timeout or Timeout	The number of seconds to wait for a connection to the server before aborting the attempt and generating an error. Valid values are between 0 and 2,147,483,647.
Data Source or Server or Address or Addr or Network Address	The name or network address of the SQL Server instance to connect to. The port number can be specified after the server name.
Initial Catalog or Database	The name of the database to use.
Integrated Security or Trusted_Connection	Specifies if the current Windows credentials are to be used to authenticate the user. The default value is **false**, meaning the UserID and Password values will be used to authenticate the user. A value of true means the curernt Windows credentials will be used. In addition to true and false, other valid values are yes (same as true), sspi (same as true), and no (same as false).
Max Pool Size	The maximum number of connections in the pool if a connection pool is employed.
Min Pool Size	The minimum number of connections in the pool if a connection pool is employed.
Password or PWD	The password to authenticate the user
Pooling	Indicates if connection pooling should be used. The valid values are true (the default), yes, false, and no.
User ID or UID	The user identifier to authenticate the user.

Table 17.3: Valid keys for SQL Server connection strings

After you compose a connection string, you can create a DbConnection object and call its Open method to open a connection. Here is code to open a connection to a SQL Server instance.

```
SqlConnection connection = new SqlConnection(conString);
try
{
```

```
        connection.Open();
        ...
}
catch (Exception e)
{
}
```

Note that the Open method may throw an exception for various reasons, including when the user does not have permissions to access the database. Also, connection pooling works seamlessly and you don't need to write code to enjoy the benefits of connection pooling.

Creating A DbCommand Object

A **DbCommand** object represents a SQL statement. To create a **DBCommand** object, instantiate the corresponding subclass and pass a **DbConnection** object to it.

There are two methods that you would normally call on a DbCommand object, ExecuteNonQuery and ExecuteReader. The signatures of the methods are as follows.

```
public abstract int ExecuteNonQuery()

public DbDataReader ExecuteReader()
```

ExecuteNonQuery is used to execute a SQL statement that does not return data, such as an INSERT, UPDATE, or DELETE statement. This method is also suitable for catalog operations like creating or deleting a table or querying the structure of a database. **ExecuteNonQuery** returns the number of rows affected by the operation.

ExecuteReader is used to execute a Select SQL statement and the method returns a DbDataReader, which allows you to read the data returned by the DbCommand.

As an example, the following code snippet creates a **SqlCommand** object that selects all rows from the customers table in a SQL Server.

```
SqlCommand cmd = new SqlCommand("SELECT * FROM customers",
        connection);
```

Creating a DbDataReader

Finally, once you have a **DbCommand** object, you can execute it by calling its ExecuteQuery method. The return value is a **DbDataReader** object.

To start accessing data in a DbDataReader, call its Read method. This method advances the data reader to the next record and returns true if there is a next record. Otherwise, it returns false.

Here is the signature of **Read**.

```
public abstract bool Read()
```

For each invocation of Read, you can access each column of the current record using the Item properties or one of the **GetXXX** methods.

The **Item** properties provide a convenient way of accessing a value. **Item** returns the value as System.Object and you can either refer to a column by index or by name. For example, this code returns the first column of the current record:

```
object value = dbDataReader[0];
```

Note that in C# you call an Item property the same way you would an array element.

This one returns the value of the last_name column in the current record.

```
object lastName = dbDataReader["last_name"];
```

Item is convenient, but it returns an object and casting might be necessary if you are going to manipulate the value further. The other option for obtainig a column value is by using one of the **GetXXX** methods on DbDataReader. Here are some of them.

```
public abstract byte GetByte(int index)

public abstract char GetChar(int index)

public abstract DateTime GetDateTime(int index)

public abstract double GetDouble(int index)

public abstract float GetFloat(int index)

public abstract short GetInt16(int index)
```

```
public abstract int GetInt32(int index)

public abstract long GetInt64(int index)

public abstract string GetString(int index)
```

For example, the following line of code calls the ExecuteReader on a
DbCommand object, iterates over all the returned rows, and prints the
value of the first column.

```
SqlDataReader dataReader = cmd.ExecuteReader();
while (dataReader.Read())
{
    Console.WriteLine(dataReader[0]);
}
```

Connecting to SQL Server Example

Now that you know the five steps to accessing a relational database using
ADO.NET, let put everything together. The code in Listing 17.1 shows
code to access the users table in a SQL Server database. To test this
example, you need access to a SQL Server that has a TestDB database
containing a users table. You also need to replace the connection string

Listing 17.1: Accessing SQL Server with ADO.NET

```
using System;
using System.Data;
using System.Data.Common;
using System.Data.SqlClient;

namespace ADONETExample1
{
    class Program
    {
        static void Main(string[] args)
        {
            // Connect to database
            string conString = "Persist Security Info=False;" +
                    "Integrated Security=true;" +
                    "Initial Catalog=TestDB;" +
                    "Server=PC\\SQLEXPRESS";
            SqlConnection connection = new SqlConnection(conString);
```

```
SqlDataReader dataReader = null;
try
{
    connection.Open();
    Console.WriteLine("Got connection");
    // Pass the connection to a command object
    SqlCommand cmd = new SqlCommand(
            "SELECT * FROM users", connection);

    // get query results
    dataReader = cmd.ExecuteReader();

    // print the CustomerID of each record
    while (dataReader.Read())
    {
        Console.WriteLine(dataReader[0]);
    }
}
catch (Exception e)
{
    Console.WriteLine(e.Message);
}
finally
{
    if (dataReader != null)
    {
        dataReader.Close();
    }

    if (connection != null)
    {
        connection.Close();
    }
}

Console.ReadKey();
        }
    }
}
```

Running this class will print the first column of the users table in the database.

Summary

ADO.NET is a .NET technology for accessing and manipulating data in various formats, including data stored in a relational database or as XML. In this chapter you learned how to access relational databases using the three most commonly used types in ADO.NET, **DbConnection**, **DbCommand**, and **DbDataReader**.

Appendix A
Visual Studio Express 2012 for Windows Desktop

Visual Studio 2012 is the latest Integrated Development Environment (IDE) from Microsoft for building web, mobile, and desktop applications. One of the versions of this software is Visual Studio Express 2012. Not as feature-packed as other versions of Visual Studio 2012, the Express edition is free forever as long as you register. The Express edition comes in several components. One of the components, Visual Studio Express 2012 for Windows Desktop, is used to build the examples accompanying this book.

This appendix provides a quick tutorial to using Visual Studio Express 2012 for Windows Desktop.

Hardware and Software Requirements

To install Visual Studio Express 2012 for Windows Desktop you need to have a computer with at least a 1.6GHz processor and a 1 GB RAM. The computer will also have 5 GB of available hard disk space. In addition, your 32-bit or 64-bit machine must have a DirectX 9-capable video card running at 1024 x 768 or higher display resolution. Most modern computers will meet these requirements.

Software-wise, your computer must run one of the following Windows operating systems:

- Windows 7 SP1 (x86 or x64)
- Windows 8 (x86 or x64)
- Windows Server 2008 R2 SP1 (x64)
- Windows Server 2012 (x64)

Download and Installation

You can download Visual Studio Express 2012 for Windows Desktop free from Microsoft's site:

```
http://www.microsoft.com/visualstudio/eng/downloads#d-express-
windows-desktop
```

To install Visual Studio Express 2012 for Windows Desktop, follow these steps.

1. Double click the binary you just downloaded. Make sure you're connected to the Internet because there are other files that need to be downloaded. You'll see the dialog like the on in Figure A.1. This dialog is the first of a series of the Setup wizard.
2. Agree to the license terms and conditions by clicking the "I agree ..." checkbox and you'll see an Install button at the bottom.
3. Click the Install button.
4. Windows will ask if you want to let the Setup program run. Click OK.
5. Now, sit tight and wait as the wizard downloads the necessary programs and preparing your system. It will take a while but don't go away. At one stage, the wizard will ask you to restart your computer. When that happens, restart it.
6. When your computer is back up, the same wizard will resume its work. Keep waiting.
7. Finally,when it's really done, you'll see the dialog like the one in Figure A.2.
8. Click LAUNCH.

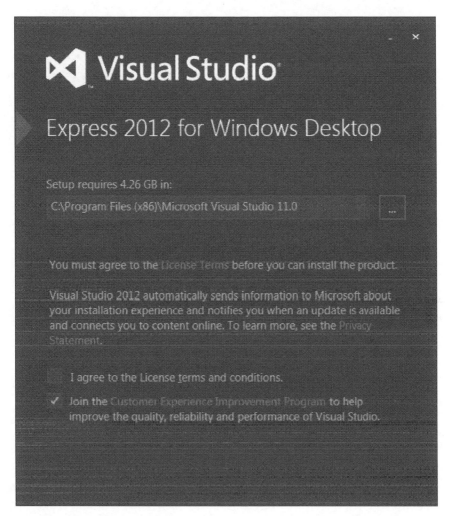

Figure A.1: The first installation dialog for Visual Studio Express 2012

Figure A.2: The last installation dialog for Visual Studio Express 2012

You'll be able to use this product for 30 days, after which you'll need to register to continue using it. If you see a dialog that prompts you to register, simply click the Cancel button to launch the software.

To register Visual Studio Express 2012, see the section "Registering" below.

When it first starts, Visual Studio Express 2012 for Windows Desktop will show a window similar to Figure A.3.

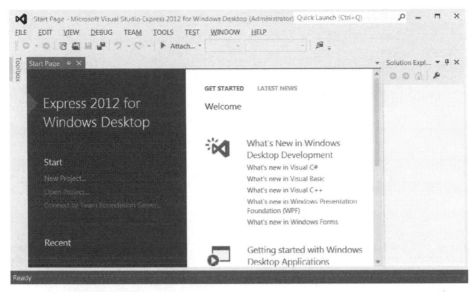

Figure A.3: Starting Visual Studio Express 2012

Congratulations. You're now ready to program.

Registering Visual Studio Express 2012

Your Visual Studio Express 2012 is free. However, Microsoft wants you to register your copy with them if you are planning to use it for more than thirty days. Don't worry, registration is free.

You know it's time to register if you get a warning dialog like that in Figure A.4 when you open Visual Stuiod Express 2012. Don't panic. You can register to get a registration key or simply close the dialog if you don't have time to register today.

To register you need a product key, which you can obtain free of charge by visiting this link and clicking the "Register now" button.

```
http://www.microsoft.com/visualstudio/eng/downloads#d-2012-express
```

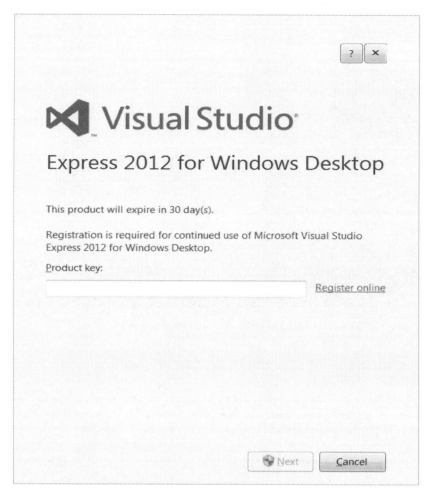

Figure A.4: Registration warning

You'll be asked to sign in with a Microsoft account. If you don't have one, you will need to create one.

Once you obtain a product key, enter it to the Product key box in the dialog in Figure A.4 and click "Register online."

Creating a Project

Visual Studio Express 2012 for Windows Desktop organizes resources in projects. Therefore, before you can create a C# class, you must first create a project. To do so, follow these steps.

1. Click **FILE**, **New Project**. The **New Project** dialog will be displayed (See Figure A.5).

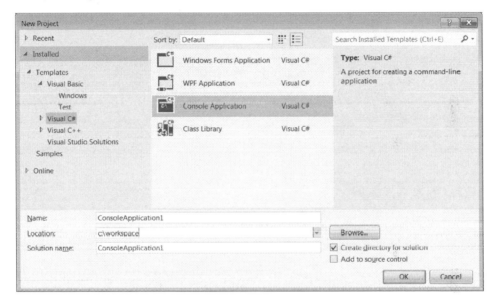

Figure A.5: The New Project dialog

2. Click Visual C# from under Installed->templates.
3. Select an application type. For this book, you will create either a Console application or a WPF application.
4. Enter a project name in the **Name** box and browse to the directory where you want to save the project's resources. Afterward, click **OK**. Visual Studio Express 2012 will create a new project plus the first class in the project. This is depicted in Figure A.6.

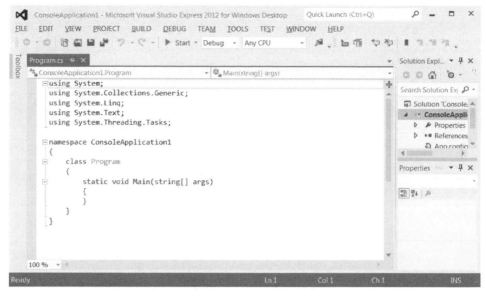

Figure A.6: A C# project

You are ready to write your code.

Creating a Class

To create a class other than that created by default by Visual Studio Express 2012 for Windows Desktop, right-click on the project name in the Solution Explorer widget. In Figure A.6 the widget is located on the right. Then, click **Add** and **Class**. You'll see the "Add New Item" dialog like the one in Figure A.7.

Enter a class name in the Name box and click **Add**. Alternatively, you can open the Add New Item dialog by pressing the shortcut Shift+Alt+C.

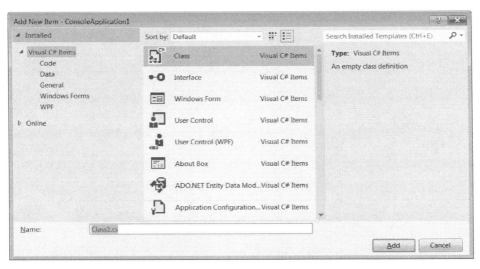

Figure A.7: The "Add New Item" Dialog

Running a Project

To run a project, press F5. Visual Studio Express 2012 for Windows Desktop will compile the project and run the class with a **Main** method. You can only have one **Main** method in a project.

Visual Studio Express 2012 for Windows Desktop will catch any compile or build errors before it runs a project.

Appendix B
Visual C# 2010 Express

One of the development tools available for C# developers is Visual C# 2010 Express. It is free even though not as feature complete as Visual Studio, which is only available for trial for 90 days.

This appendix provides a quick tutorial to using Visual C# 2010 Express. If you're using Windows 7 or Windows 8, consider using the latest IDE from Microsoft, Visual Studio Express 2012.

Hardware and Software Requirements

To install Visual C# 2010 Express you need to have a computer with at least a 1.6GHz processor and a 1 GB RAM (if it is a 32 bit machine) or 2 GB RAM (it it is a 64 bit machine). The computer will also have 3 GB of available hard disk space.

As for the software requirements, your computer must run one of the following Windows operating systems:

- Windows XP (x86) with Service Pack 3, all editions except Starter Edition
- Windows Vista (x86 or x64) with Service Pack 2, all editions except Starter Edition
- Windows 7 (x86 or x64)
- Windows Server 2003 (x86 or x64) with Service Pack 2
- Windows Server 2003 R2 (x86 or x64)
- Windows Server 2008 (x86 or x64) with Service Pack 2
- Windows Server 2008 R2 (x64)

Download and Installation

You can download Visual C# 2010 Express free from Microsoft's site.

```
http://www.microsoft.com/visualstudio/en-us/products/2010-
editions/express
```

Scroll down until you see the Visual C# 2010 Express link and click it. You'll be redirected to another page with links to install the English version or a version in another language. Currently, the supported languages are English, Spanish, Italian, French, German, Russian, Chinese, Japanese, and Korean. Select your language and click the Install Now button.

When you click the Install Now button, you'll see a dialog box. Here Microsoft tries to lure you to install Visual Studio 2010 Professional instead. Be strong and insist on Visual C# 2010 Express and save the binary file.

To install Visual C# 2010 Express, follow these steps.

1. Double click the binary you just downloaded. Make sure you're connected to the Internet because there are other files that need to be downloaded. You'll see a dialog like the one in Figure B.1. This is the first dialog of a series of the Setup wizard.
2. Click Next. You'll see the License Terms as in the following dialog. Read the terms and if you agree, click "I have read and accept the license terms" radio.
3. Click Next again. In the dialog box that follows, you'll be offered to download Microsoft SQL Server 2008 Express. It is a good idea to download this product if you do not have it installed. So, click the check box if you want to install it or leave it unchecked if you don't.
4. Click Next again. The Setup wizard will display the last dialog before it starts installation. Here you can choose the install folder and view the list of components that will be downloaded and installed. By default, the wizard will try to install them under C:\Program Files\Microsoft Visual Studio 10.0. You can select a different folder if you wish. See Figure B.2.

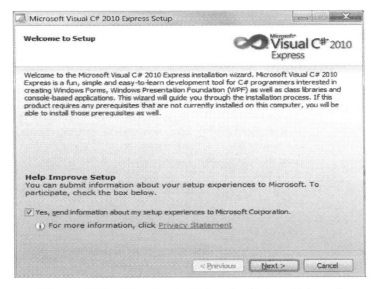

Figure B.1: The first dialog in Setup Wizard

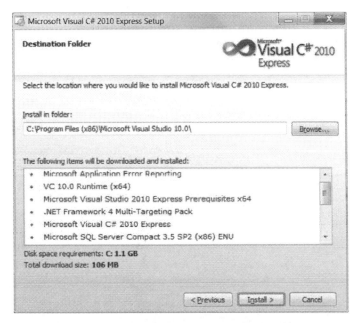

Figure B.2: Selecting an installation folder

5. You're ready to go. Click Install to proceed with installation. The next dialog shows the progress of the installation. See Figure B.3.

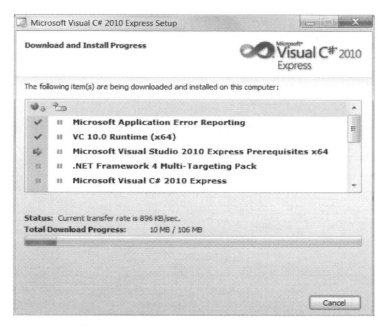

Figure B.3: Installation progress

6. If Visual C# 2010 Express was installed successfully, you'll see a dialog like the one in Figure B.4.

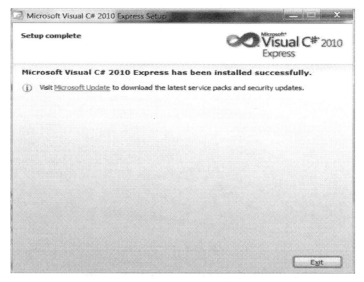

Figure B.4: Installation complete

7. Click on Exit to quit the Setup.

Congratulations. You can now start using Visual C# 2010 Express. Launch the application and you'll see a window similar to that in Figure B.5.

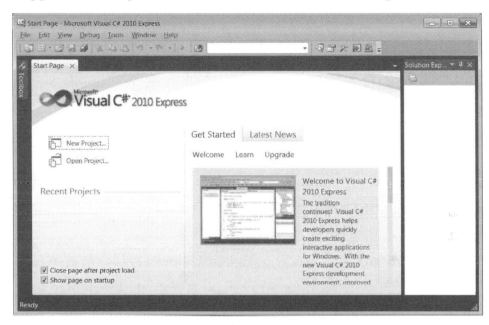

Figure B.5: Starting Visual C# 2010 Express

Registering Your Visual C# 2010 Express

Your Visual C# 2010 Express is free. However, Microsoft wants you to register your copy with them if you are planning to use it for more than thirty days. Don't worry, registration is free.

If you open Visual C# 2010 Express and you get a warning dialog like that in Figure B.6, don't panic. You can register to get a registration key or simply close the dialog if you don't have time to register today.

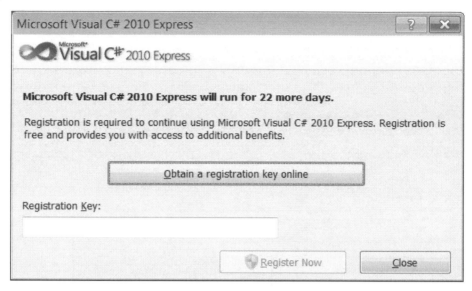

Figure B.6: Registration warning

Creating a Project

Visual C# 2010 Express organizes resources in projects. Therefore, before you can create a C# class, you must first create a project. To do so, follow these steps.

1. Click the **File** menu and select **New Project**. The **New Project** dialog will be displayed.
2. Click Visual C# from under Installed->templates.
3. Select an application type. For this book, you will create either a Console application or a WPF application.
4. Enter a project name in the **Name** box and browse to the directory where you want to save the project's resources. Afterward, click **OK**. Visual C# 2010 Express will create a new project plus the first class in the project.

You are ready to write your code.

Creating a Class

To create a class other than that created by default by Visual C# 2010, right-click on the project name in the Solution Explorer widget. Then, click **Add** and **Class**. You'll see the "Add New Item" dialog.

Enter a class name in the Name box and click **Add**. Alternatively, you can open the Add New Item dialog by pressing the shortcut Shift+Alt+C.

Running a Project

To run a project, press F5. Visual C# 2010 Express will compile the project and run the class with a **Main** method. Visual C# 2010 Express will catch any compile or build errors before it runs a project.

Appendix C
SQL Server 2012 Express

Microsoft SQL Server is one of the most popular relational database servers today and this appendix explains how to download and install the free version of this widely used software, SQL Server 2012 Express.

Downloading SQL Server 2012 Express

The SQL Server products can be downloaded from this site:

`http://www.microsoft.com/en-us/sqlserver/get-sql-server/try-it.aspx`

Scroll down until you see the link to download the free SQL Server 2012 Express version. Click the Download button next to the product and select the 32bit or 64 bit version.

Save the installation .exe file in your hard disk.

Installing SQL Server 2012 Express

To install SQL Server 2012 Express, follow these steps.

1. Double-click on the installation file you downloaded. You will see a dialog that looks like Figure C.1.

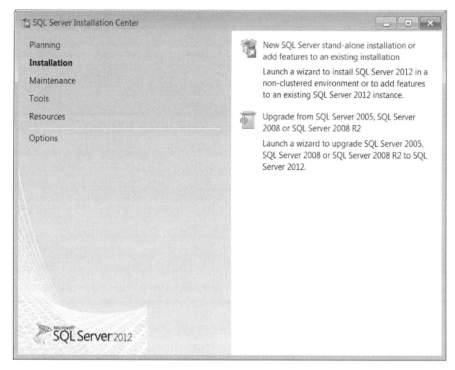

Figure C.1: Starting the installation process

2. On the right window, click **New SQL Server stand-alone installation**.
3. In the next window, check the **I accept the license terms** checkbox.
4. Click Next. The Feature Selection window, shown in Figure C.2, will open.

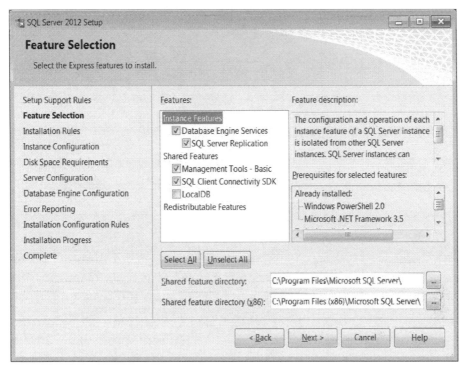

Figure C.2: The Feature Selection window

5. Accept the default and then click **Next**.
6. The next window is the Installation Rules window that list all components required. (See Figure C.3.)
   If one or more components failed, click on the Failed link. There will be information on the failed component and you need to resolve any failed component before installation can continue. For example, Figure C.3 shows a failed component

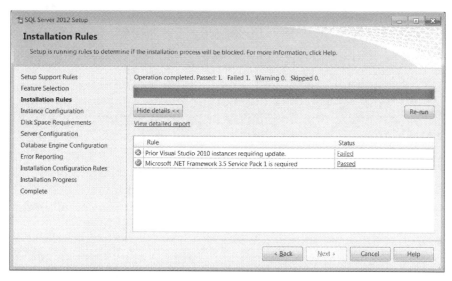

Figure C.3: The Installation Rules window

7. After you resolve all failed components, click the Back button to go back to the Feature Selection window. Then in the Feature Selection window, click Next to try again. If all components installed correctly, the Installation Rules window will be skipped and you will see the Instance Configuration window, as shown in Figure C.4.

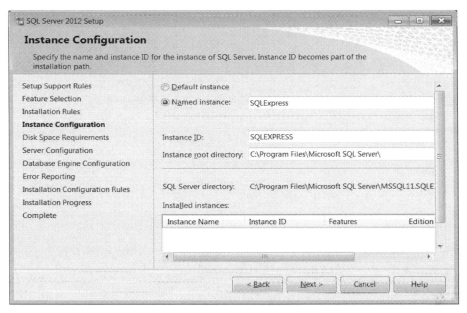

Figure C.4: The Instance Configuration window

8. Again, accept the default and click Next. You will see the Server Configuration window like the one in Figure C.5.

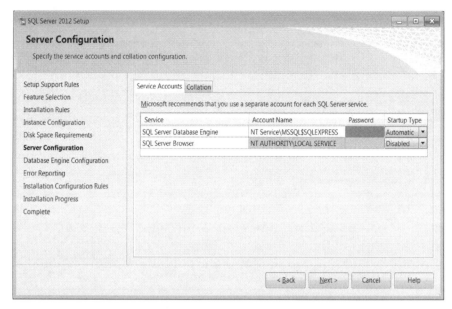

Figure C.5: The Server Configuration window

9. Click Next and you'll see the Database Engine Configuration window like the one in Figure C.6.

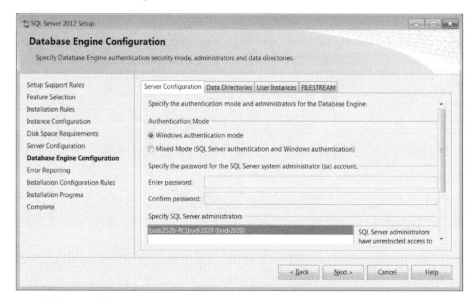

Figure C.6: The Database Engine Configuration window

10.Click Next again. The next window that will show is the Error Reporting window. (See Figure C.7.)

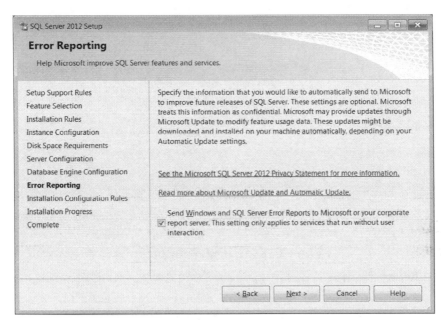

Figure C.7: The Error Reporting window

11.Click Next again and installation will start. The process will be shown in the Installation Progress window like that in Figure C.8.

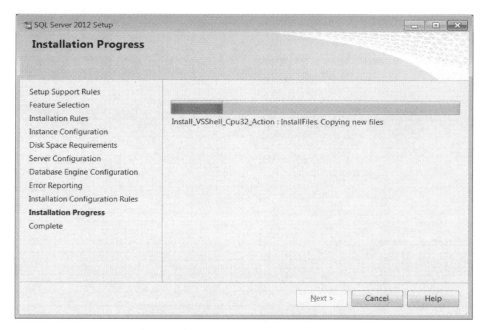

Figure C.8: Installation progress

12. If all is well, the Installation Progress window will disappear and be replaced by another window that explains that installation is complete (See Figure C.9.) Examine the components installed and click Close. You'll be back to the SQL Server Installation Center window. Close that too.

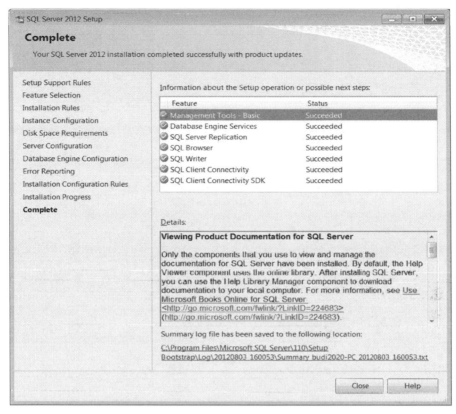

Figure C.9: The Complete window

The installation wizard will create a shortcut to Microsoft SQL Server Management Studio under the Microsoft SQL Server 2012 menu. You use this management program to manage your database objects, such as creating databases and tables and populates them with data.

Connecting to SQL Server and Creating A Database

You use Microsoft SQL Server Management Studio to create a database. To start managing a database, run the management program. When it opens,

SQL Server Management Studio will prompt you to connect to a database server. Figure C.10 shows the Login window.

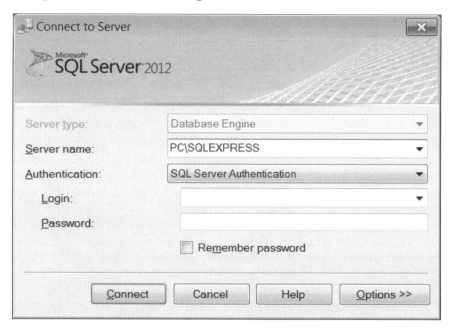

Figure C.10: The Login window of SQL Server Management Studio

The first thing to do is to connect to an instance of SQL Server. One should have been created when you installed SQL Server. Therefore, select a server in the **Server name** field.

To connect, you need to login, either using Windows authentication or SQL Server authentication. If you're using the former, click the Connect button. If you're using the latter, type in your login name and password and click Connect.

Figure C.11 shows the main window of SQL Server Management Studio after you successfully logged in. You should see in the Object Explorer pane the SQL Server instance you're currently logged in to.

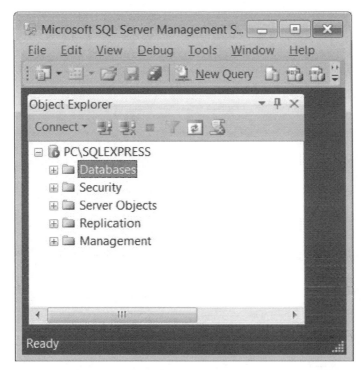

Figure C.11: The main window of SQL Server Management Studio

To create a database, right-click on the Databases folder in Object Explorer and click on New Database. The New Database window will open. Type in a name and click the Add button. Your new database will appear under the Databases folder in Object Explorer.

Index

Made in the USA
Charleston, SC
27 August 2016